OVERCOMING WOUNDEDNESS

Lessons From The Life of Joseph

SALLY MEREDITH

ISBN 978-1-63575-675-3 (Paperback)
ISBN 978-1-63575-676-0 (Digital)

Christian Faith Publishing, Inc.
296 Chestnut Street
Meadville, PA 16335
www.christianfaithpublishing.com

Printed in the United States of America

ENDORSEMENTS

We all need a gentle voice that is wiser. Sally speaks with wisdom and she is gentle as she leads us to greater understanding and application of the truth found in the old story of Joseph. We have been captive to incomplete knowledge. We have been exiled to superficial stories. She takes us deeper not only into the awareness of Joseph, but of ourselves, and our families. We have all come from families, yet we have failed to see ourselves in this one family's story. Lord, forgive us. And, thank you Sally for guiding us into deeper truth of this Biblical story and ourselves and our genesis.

Dixie Fraley Keller,
Author of *The Widow's Workbook*

Sally has been our friend for 50 years, and we have been blessed by her enthusiasm for teaching God's Word and her ability to connect the truth of Scripture with those sitting under her. Even the most Biblically illiterate can understand the story of Joseph through her definitions and explanations. This book is for everyone who has ever struggled to understand the workings of God. Sally applies the goodness and sovereignty of God and encourages us to live in the larger story of His redemptive work in our lives and in the world.

Dr. Barry and Mary Leventhal
Distinguished Senior Professor
Southern Evangelical Seminary

Sally Meredith has crafted a solidly biblical book that reminds us of the truth about God in the midst of betrayal, injustice, woundedness, and suffering. This book is a salve that brings healing for the wounds of life.

Dennis Rainey, Author, Speaker,
Co-Founder of FamilyLife
Radio host of FamilyLife Today

Sally Meredith is a gifted student and teacher of the Old Testament, and her well-crafted portrayal of the dramatic story of Joseph *in Overcoming Woundedness* is rich in analysis and application. In it she develops an honest and biblically accurate depiction of wounds and betrayals in families, friendships and the workplace, and shows how wounded people wound other people. She skillfully demonstrates the purposes of God in trials and the way He sovereignly uses injustice and unfairness in a fallen world to bring His people to the point of giving up self to find their true self in Jesus. The insights on dealing with bitterness and the power of forgiveness alone are more than worth the price of this book.

Kenneth Boa
Author, Speaker
President of Reflections Ministries

Sally Meredith's book, *Overcoming Woundedness,* is not just about the life of Joseph, but also about the journey we all experience in the wounds of life and the questions raised. She has experiential and practical wisdom about life with God and what it means to relate to Him in the power of the Holy Spirit. Her refreshing insights into the truths of grace, love, and faith are of great encouragement to all seeking deeper bonding with God and others.

David A English
Cru, Leadership Development
Author, *The Eternal Bond* and *Phases of Life Studies*

Sally Meredith shares lessons from a lifetime of study and application of God's Word to personal woundedness. If you are dealing with the pain and anguish of being emotionally wounded, this book will provide new perspective, encouragement and real help.

Sherry Crater, Pastor's wife, teacher and speaker

In Sally's fresh work on a familiar character, she honestly and adeptly shows how the toughest wounds to deal with are those inflicted by friends and family. We all have felt the sting from those we love. As Sally walks us through the life of Joseph, it's easy to fall in step with her as she navigates us through struggles and into a hope that heals.

Brian and Jen Goins,
Authors, speakers for FamilyLife.

Like Joseph, many of us dream of greatness without knowing what it is or the cost involved in attaining it. As Sally Meredith probes this saints' painful journey to spiritual significance, we are challenged to look at our wounds through the grid of Joseph's life, helping us gain a fresh perspective on them through God's eyes. Her very personal style makes you feel as if you are sharing an intimate conversation with her over a cup of coffee. Having experienced the blessing of leading a group through her study of Ruth, we can't wait to take them on this next spiritual journey.

Rev. Bill and Ann Parkinson
SageWorks Pastor
Fellowship Bible Church, Little Rock, Arkansas

I feel like shouting to everyone, "Don't miss reading and devouring this book!" Your anxieties will be lifted as this study points out that "God's plan for your life cannot be thwarted by Satan or mankind no matter the circumstances or obstacles put in the way." Sally provides a wonderfully fresh perspective regarding the years of wrestling mentally and emotionally that Joseph must have experienced. As you read, you will be assured that God is at work on your behalf as He was on Joseph's behalf to bring about an outcome that will astound you and will honor Him. Read and be blessed.

Dr. Gordon and Marcy Klenck,
Teachers, speakers, trainers
Senior Staff of Cru Ministry

In OVERCOMING WOUNDEDNESS, Sally Meredith conveys the loving hand of an omniscient God through our pain and struggles, as He conforms us in the likeness of Christ. Sally's depth of understanding of God's hand in the life of Joseph and many others who walked by faith, with her 50 years of personal struggle and ministry, provides a rich and rewarding read for all who yearn for our hope in Christ on this earth as He prepares us to be with Him for eternity.

Robert Pittenger
Member of Congress
North Carolina, 9th District

DEDICATION

To the wounded among us

If you have ever been wounded by a family
member, this book is for you.

If you have ever been wounded in the
workplace, this book is for you.

If you have ever been wounded by a friend, this book is for you.

ACKNOWLEDGMENTS

Special thanks to a special group of women who met weekly to give advise and rearrange content: Ann Conway, Janice Bostick, Pat Gibbs, Lynn Wray, Jennie Wyatt, Tiffany Haines, Kathryn Ruby, Meg Henry, Margaret McKinney, Nita Youngblood. You are loved and appreciated.

Thanks to two special women who took "their women" through the manuscript, giving wonderful advice and corrections: Dixie Fraley Keller and Ann Conway. Thanks to my editors, especially Ginger Thomas, at Christian Faith Publishers for your help getting this book to the finish line.

A special thanks to my children and their spouses: Todd and Sara, Scott and Carmen, Brandon and Kathryn, and Brad and Tiffany, who constantly show me in more ways than you know that God has arms of love manifested in your lives. Thank you for producing for me those amazing gifts of grandchildren. My quiver is rejoicing.

And to my husband of 50 years – thank you for believing in me and for your undying faith love, which you exhibit "almost" daily. We have laughed and cried and rejoiced in our years together – oh how thankful I am for you.

Thank you to God for reminding me during the writing and editing process of this book on wounding that You still have work to do in my own life. This process never ends but is producing glory for Your Kingdom. Thank You.

CONTENTS

FOREWORD

Although Sally's insight from God's perspective and historical detail is scholarly, her practical understanding of living in our humanness is what cuts deep into the hearts of serious followers of the risen Christ. In *Overcoming Woundedeness*, she gives us real-world application into how we can better walk with Jesus as God orders our steps to accomplish our greatest good and His greatest glory.

By following the life of Joseph and God's hedge of grace around him, we are given great hope no matter the pain, betrayal, or lack of love from those who should love us best… our family. I am reminded that God's agenda and His glorious ways and plans are accomplished according to His timetable. Those of us who have placed our hope in Christ can be confident that the gates of hell will not stop His conquering march.

Learning from Joseph's wounds can save us from some of the pain we will inevitably go through in this life as we learn that God's ways are higher than our ways. If we apply the truths Sally discovered in this marvelous story of real people living in a hurtful environment, we will experience God's daily grace in a much deeper way. Our Father applies His abounding grace in molding each of us into the image of His beloved Son and is working to prepare us to rule with our Lord Jesus for eternity. As we see in the life of Joseph, sometimes this "soul surgery" takes time.

Sally's great insight in this book can be summed up with this: The safest place in our Christian human existence is to be in the center of God's loving will for our life.

This rings true even if it involves us carrying our cross as modeled by Christ who said, "not My will, Father, but Your will." Jesus knew the heart of His Father, and knew that He could trust the will and way of God Almighty. The guiding principle of these marvelous stories and Sally's God ordained insight is that our Father's way, timing, and results are always for our good and His glory.

Sally's whole intent is that if Joseph can endure what he went through, so can she, so can I, and so can you. The same God that ordered Joseph's steps is the same God we trust and follow today. God has not changed. His motive is still pure love for each of us. Our fight is not to quit before the Master Artist completes His masterpiece in our lives. His driving agenda is passionately committed to "transforming us into the likeness and image of Jesus" (Romans 8:29).

Sally's understanding of Joseph's life will minister to all who have been bought out of the slave market of our kingdoms and into the Church. The Body of Christ needs to know and walk in the truth of this book. For those who long to know Christ better and find themselves in the pit of human despair, this book is a must read. It will bless you as it moves you closer to Your Father's heart.

John Maisel,
Author, Founder and Chairman Emeritus
East/West Ministries International

WHY ANOTHER BOOK ABOUT JOSEPH?

I am going to take you on a journey into one of the most beloved stories of all time. The ancient story of Joseph has been told to countless generations by millions of parents, ministers, and Bible teachers on every continent of the world and in every era of time. No wonder Sunday school classes, missionaries, churches, and leaders of nations study his life. Men, women, and children want to be like him. Kings and rulers try to emulate him. If you want a fairy tale ending, well, this is it. *"And they lived happily ever after."*

Joseph practically jumps from the pages of history into our modern-day world to teach us what human nature is like, both the struggles and the victories. We get to take a peek into the inner man, into the heart of Joseph. We get to see what God saw.

The book of Genesis lists hundreds of names but with very few does the author stop and elaborate. Why is this one man given so much space? What can we learn from a man born centuries ago and how will that affect our lives in the modern-day world? Taking the lessons from Joseph, I am struck anew how my life can help change those around me. I first must learn the lessons Joseph learned—the hard way. I too learn the hard way. That's the beauty of this story. His life was filled with trauma and triumph. He will plunge to the deepest humiliation in a dingy prison cell, and he will scale the heights of power and fame that none of us even think possible.

What I will lay out in this book is the story I think Joseph would want to tell, and it is this: Joseph was no different than we are. I have heard a different story all my life about Joseph. I assumed that God gave him special insight into why God does what He does. And I've been told by numerous Bible teachers that he simply looked at life like God looks at life and, therefore, could make the unbelievable statements to his brothers that he did. That perspective certainly didn't apply to me because I couldn't be that "godly." Do you feel the same?

As I read between the lines and hear Joseph's testimony from his own lips, I am left with a different story all together. Joseph didn't have a more integral connection to God than we do. He came from a dysfunction, the same as we are. He struggled with the hurts that were heaped upon him. Did he question? Did he think God was being unfair? Was Joseph like us or was he above us?

If we look at a life like Joseph's and say he was different, we have not read this right. If we say he had a perspective that we cannot attain, we are mistaken. He would be the first to tell us his own shortcomings.

Most teachers of the Bible put him on a pedestal. This book will take him off that pedestal and put him squarely where you and I live. I believe that's where he would want to be, alongside us, cheering us on as we go through life's hard lessons. As we peer into his heart, hopefully we will find our own.

The question we have to answer by the end of the book is this: *How did God take an arrogant seventeen-year-old and turn him into a man of faith who visualized God's perspective instead of wallowing in the wounds of humanity? How does his life pertain to mine?*

Now let's jump into his life. Hang on for the ride!

Introduction
Setting the Stage

Of all the books ever written in history, the Bible is the most unique and perplexing. It is intriguing and life changing. We can read it again and again, yet never fully comprehending its content. It is an amazing book. It's brilliant and inspired. When reading the Bible we find ourselves weeping and laughing, convicted, yet drawn in. Each time we open its pages it appears *new*! What kind of book is this?

It is the only book in all of human history that a person can enjoy like a novel, contemplate like a devotional book, read like a story, study like theology, devour like history, and tear apart like literature. We can read it daily, monthly, yearly, never tiring of its pages. It's like no other book in all of history.

It guides, convicts, inspires, and humbles us. It's the only book that offers hope and life change. It offers redemption and forgiveness. It offers eternal life if we accept its terms. What other book can do all of this?

The Bible comprises sixty-six books written over a time span of fifteen hundred years by thirty-nine different authors. Yet it is written as one book with one dominate theme: the Messiah and the forgiveness of sins. The Old Testament (OT) predicts the coming of Messiah Jesus. The New Testament (NT) gives the account of His coming and predicts His second coming. The Bible not only gives lessons from the past, it has visions for the future. It is *His* story from cover to cover. What an amazing book!

Contrasts in Scripture

Contrasts abound in the Bible. One of the most looming is the contrast between *God and us.* He is God, and we are not. He controls, and we do not. He loves with a perfect love while ours is shallow at best. He loves us when we are unlovable. He does the bending, and we break. Who is this amazing God that speaks to us through His Written Word? He is the God of the Bible and the stories He tells are His stories.

Understanding History

History is what makes the present knowable and gives life meaning. I believe that's why God in His sovereignty gave us so much history. We look at the past. We study people, wars, and famous authors. We try to put the pieces of the puzzle together. We can never get enough!

For me, the first book of the Bible, Genesis, is like that. I have studied this book all my adult life. I have taught it, memorized parts of it, and have been moved by its lessons. Every time I read it, something new pops out of its pages. This has been especially true while writing and contemplating the life of Joseph.

After years of speaking about Joseph at women's retreats, I thought I knew this story well. But while writing I have been impacted in deeper ways as I have torn apart, verse by verse, this amazing story in the Old Testament. The lessons I learned years ago from the life of Joseph have impacted me again as I have experienced wounding from a different perspective.

The Puzzle Box

Before we get into the back story of Joseph, we must stop and talk about the puzzle that is the Old Testament. Many people don't read the whole Bible, or they pick and choose what appeals to them (like Psalms and Proverbs) and skip most of the historical narrative. For sure, they skip over genealogies, not knowing why these lists of people are in the Scriptures at all. When coming to genealogies most people say, "Who cares?" and skim right through them.

If you grew up in church, you may have learned a few fascinating stories from the Old Testament: Adam and Eve, Moses crossing the Red Sea, Jonah being swallowed by a great fish, Daniel in the lion's den. And that's our concept of the Old Testament. Were these isolated stories, or was there a purpose? Is there a pattern? Why is the Old Testament laid out like it is? How did it get that way? Is there connection within its pages?

If I told you to go to the store and get a puzzle of the Old Testament, what would you look for? Would you go to a "puzzle-piece bin" and just start picking out pieces? That's what we do in reality when reading the Old Testament. For the most part we see the Old Testament as a bunch of puzzle pieces that make no sense. They are scattered stories, each having a lesson to learn, but with no connection between the stories. God does provide the picture on the cover, if we are willing to find it.

Below are my thoughts of what the "picture" on the top of the box might look like. Look at the drawing. A banana has fruit on the inside and peelings on the outside. The peelings are purposeful as they protect and preserve the fruit.

There are two trains of thought running throughout the Bible: the Messiah and the people of faith.

The Messiah

The fruit of the banana will be the Messianic lineage of Jesus Christ. The peelings will be people of *faith*. Some will be in the lineage of Christ, while others will not. Many of these people will be listed in Hebrews 11, which is a chapter on the people of faith in Old Testament times.

From Adam to Jesus, the OT follows His genealogy through centuries to the beginning of the NT. First Chronicles gives the genealogy of all the tribes of Israel. Through that book we can follow the line of the Messiah from Adam to David's two sons Nathan and Solomon, who will be Jesus's lineage through both his parents as told in Matthew 1 (Joseph's lineage) and Luke 4 (Mary's lineage).

The earliest strands of the Messianic idea speak of an offspring who will undo the work of the Evil One.

> *And I will put enmity*
> *Between you and the woman,*
> *And between your seed and her seed;*
> *He shall bruise you on the head,*
> *And you shall bruise him on the heel.*
> *(Gen. 3:15)*

The Messiah will descend from Abraham (Gen. 17:6–7), Jacob (Gen. 35:11), and Judah.

> *The scepter shall not depart from Judah,*
> *Nor the ruler's staff from between his feet,*
> *Until Shiloh comes,*
> *And to him shall be the obedience of the peoples.*
> *(Gen. 49:10)*

There is a promise of a lasting dynasty for David

> *Your house and your kingdom shall endure before*
> *Me forever; your throne shall be established forever.*
> *(2 Sam. 7:16)*
> (Ps. 2:8, 72:8–17; Gen. 22:18; Isa. 9:6–7,
> 11:1–10, 42:1–9)

People of Faith Form an Unending Line to our Present Day:
Believing without Seeing – A Relay Race

The OT defines faith and follows not only the bloodline of Messiah, but the faith-line to the New Testament and beyond to our day. Some of the same men and women will be in both lines, but there are a lot of names in the faith line that are not part of the Messianic genealogy.

Hebrews 11 has no ending as it will continue long past the New Testament times throughout all ages to our present age. It's likened to a relay race where *people of faith pass the baton to others* who will pass it to others, etc., until the last person on earth who accepts Christ as Savior finishes the race.

The purpose of defining faith in Hebrews 11 is that it is *incomplete* and, therefore, continues into our day. You and I hope to be listed as people of faith in our lifetimes. Faith in God the Creator, spoken of in the Bible, is our hope, our joy, our peace, and our salvation. God is building His Kingdom through His people of *faith*. None of us will receive the garland (prize) for a life well lived until the race is over. That's why there is a great cloud of witnesses cheering us on in our race. They, along with us, will receive the prize together.

It's all about us! We have the baton, and we pass it to others. Look at these verses out of Hebrews 11:

Now faith is the assurance of things hoped for, the conviction of things not seen. For by it the men of old gained approval. (vs. 1–2)

And without faith it is impossible to please Him, for he who comes to God must believe that He is and that He is a rewarder of those who seek Him. (vs. 6)

And all these, having gained approval through their faith, did not receive what was promised, *because God had provided something better for us, so that apart from us they would not be made perfect. (vs. 39–40)*

Therefore, since we have so great a cloud of witnesses surrounding us (OT people of faith, NT people of faith, modern day people of faith), let us also lay aside every encumbrance and the sin which so easily entangles us, and let us run with endurance the race that is set before us, fixing our eyes on Jesus, the author and perfecter of faith, who for the joy set before Him endured the cross, despising the shame, and has sat down at the right hand of the throne of God. For consider Him who has endured such hostility by sinners against Himself, so that you will not grow weary and lose heart. (Heb. 12:1–3)

In Appendix 3, the entire chapter of Hebrews 11 is printed for you. As you can surmise, this is not a complete list of people in the Old Testament who lived by faith. *These are examples of people of faith.* Notice that some, but not all, are in the Messianic lineage. Others are *"peelings with a purpose,"* such as Joseph, Moses, Joshua, the judges, Samuel, and the prophets. The Messianic lineage will be emphasized for you.

God has included both lines (Messianic and Faith) for our enjoyment and our learning. Our task is to determine why they were included and what practical application they may have for our lives.

All People Are One Race

There is only one race of people: the human race. Throughout the world today we are governed by language. In Mexico, Spanish is spoken. Greek is spoken in Greece. In Africa, numerous dialects. In Germany, German. English was spoken in England, paving the way for America. We naturally gather around people who speak our native tongue. That way, the world is divided by language and culture. It was then; it is now.

> *And He made from one man every nation of mankind to live on all the face of the earth, having determined their appointed times and the boundaries of their habitation. (Acts 17:26)*

We have different languages, cultures, and skin coloring. But we all come from Adam and Noah. Therefore, we are *one* race of people. Satan has distorted the issue of "race" by having us focus on skin color. We have different cultures, not different races. The issue of race today is a mammoth attack of Satan who tries to divide and cause dissension.

After the flood, Noah's three sons were divided into different cultures and languages. An example of "peelings" would be Japeth and Ham, Noah's sons. If you are from European and Asian descent, you are from the tribe of Japeth. If you are African or some Middle

Eastern, you are from the tribe of Ham. The Bible is about the lineage of Shem. The promises of God, however, are for *all* mankind.

Shem's Lineage Is Predominant in Scripture

It's Noah's son Shem whose genealogy is key to Old Testament scripture. It's through him that the people Israel come forth. From the third chapter of Genesis, humanity was promised a "seed" that would eventually crush the head of Satan, who is personified as evil in the world. This promised seed is the Messiah spoken of throughout the whole of Old Testament writings. He is mentioned on and off for thousands of years.

Through Shem will come the Abrahamic line of Isaac and Jacob. Jacob's lineage will be narrowed to Judah and is then followed throughout the rest of the Old Testament writings leading from King David to the time of Jesus Christ, the Messiah, revealed in the New Testament.

So do you see the top of the box more clearly now? Both the Old and New Testaments are all about the *Messiah*. The OT predicts His coming; and the NT confirms his life, death, and resurrection. It's all about Him. Every book, every story, and every era of time points to Him. Whenever God deviates from stories about the promised Messianic line, the purpose is for our *faith*. Joseph will fit into the category of faith.

Ancient Names

A name reflects character, lineage, and may be even identified with events and eras. By just stating a name, the story is pictured in our minds. It was so in ancient times; it is true today. Each of us has a story connected to our name. We will find that in Scripture, names have significant meanings that often tell the actual story of the event. Ann Voskamps in her book *One Thousand Gifts* states:

Naming is Edenic…God, in the beginning, first speaks a name and lets what is come into existence. This naming is how the first emptiness of space fills the naming of light and land and sky. The first man's first task is to name. Adam names creatures…naming offers the gift of recognition…to name is to learn the language of Paradise…to name it is to solve a mystery.

Because names play a defining role in the testimony of Joseph, we must introduce this interesting sidelight of Old Testament history. Names are not afterthoughts in Scripture. Often names were pivotal in telling a story. The life of Joseph is no exception. If we miss the meaning of the names of his sons, we will miss the whole story! Eastern culture, unlike western culture, thinks in terms of pictures or visuals to ponder. Names are amazingly "stories in picture form."

Names come from different sources:

1) God gave names.
2) God changed names.
3) Parents gave names that told their story.
4) Cities and nations are given meaning-laden names.
5) God has numerous names defining His characteristics.

God starts off by naming everything created. He named the first man *Adam*, meaning "dust, dirt, earth."

Adam gave the first woman a name, *Eve*, which means "mother of all living."

Abel was the first child to be listed in Hebrews 11:4, the chapter on faith. His name literally means "breath," "breathing spirit," or "vapor." Even though Cain killed Abel, it says about him that "he still speaks." What does he speak? He speaks of faith, which characterizes men and women who trust in God as their Savior, knowing that in the flesh we cannot be made righteous.

Seth (vs. 4:25) means "anointed, compensation, or appointed." With all three of these definitions, we can tell the story that Seth was the appointed one from whom Messiah's bloodline would come.

Noah means "rest" or "comfort." Really? What was so restful and comforting as a worldwide flood? The account of the flood is one of the darkest stories in human history. Can you imagine preaching day after day to your friends and *none* of them become believers? And then to enter the ark, God closing the door, and you have to hear the sounds of floodwaters hitting the hull and hear the screams of the people trying to find a way to get into this massive ship? I am convinced that God wanted the windows only at the top so that Noah and his family couldn't "see" what was going on outside. This is not a children's story. It is a tragic story of the rebellion of mankind and the severe judgment of a Sovereign God.

Noah's son *Shem* (vs. 10:21–11:32) actually means "name."

Everything and everybody has a name. It's what makes us human. Our name gives us identity. Nothing exists without a name—no human, no plant, no animal. Even the stars all have names.

The Patriarchs: Joseph's Family Tree

Abraham is the great-grandfather of Joseph (Gen. 11:27–20:18). Abraham was called *the first Hebrew*. It was in believing that God changed his name from Abram (father) to Abraham (father of a multitude).

Isaac, grandfather of Joseph, means "laughter" (Gen. 17:17, 17:21, 18:12, 21:6) because of his unusual birth. God spoke the name of Isaac one year prior to his birth. Abraham and Sarah were one hundred and ninety respectively and well past the point of conception! Yet she got pregnant one year after an angel told her she would. She laughed. Who wouldn't have? Therefore, Isaac means laughter.

Jacob, twin of Esau, (Gen. 25:19–50). Jacob is Joseph's father. Jacob would carry on the Hebrew (Jewish) lineage and would have twelve sons. Esau would become the father of the Arab nations, along with Ishmael, Abraham's first son by Hagar.

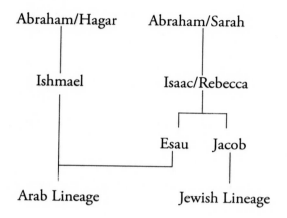

Questions for Introductory Chapter:

1) Name the two trains of thought throughout the Old Testament.

   a)

   b)

2) Why is it important to study Biblical genealogy?

3) Why is it important to know the meaning of names in Scripture?

4) Do you know the meaning of your name and why you were given that name?

CHAPTER 1

DYSFUNCTIONAL FAMILIES: MALE SIDE

You might not think that you came from a dysfunctional family, but you did. We all did. Every family since the dawn of time is dysfunctional because we came from the family of Adam. I'm sure when Adam and Eve sinned they never thought one son would murder another son! When they ate of the tree of good and evil, did they know how many arguments they would have or did they watch in dismay at the sibling rivalry and dissension that came into their lives and then into the family tree of humanity?

My family of origin certainly had characteristics of dysfunction. I brought those same dysfunctions into my marriage and then to my own children. I didn't mean to. I didn't want to. But I did.

My parents came together during the Great Depression in our nation. Mom met Dad when she was only fourteen years old. Dad played in a band and was seventeen years old. They dated a number of years until Mom was seventeen, and then they married. Four pregnancies came in rapid succession, with the first ending in miscarriage and the second a full-term baby, who died at birth. Wow, times were tough for these two young inexperienced people struggling to make ends meet and watching babies die. Mom and Dad lived with Dad's parents, not being able to afford a house of their own. Times were very lean and bleak.

Adding to the trauma of their lives, my sister and I survived our own premature births. Many people were living hand-to-mouth in a culture that was not the American dream. World War II broke out. My dad was inducted into the Army but never served either in Europe or the Pacific. He acquired a skin disease and was in the army hospital till the end of the war.

My father was a man who had, shall we say, a very colorful language! Every other word seemed like a swear word, but it was the way the men in his family talked. I don't remember a conversation as I was growing up that wasn't sprinkled heavily with words that no child should hear. Of course, if my sister or I said any of those words, our mouth had to be washed out with soap. Go figure, my dad could and did say what he pleased. But if we did the same, the discipline came out. What hypocrisy! My dad was an angry man, every day of his life. He was there, but he was passive toward me and my sister. We longed for a dad who loved us and told us so. That was the dysfunction I grew up with.

* * *

Census data, February 4, 2013, states that one-third of American children (fifteen million) are being raised without a father. Five million live without a mother. (A total of twenty million children live in single-parent homes.) These statistics raises an alarm. One out of every three families lives without a dad in the home. For girls, the lack of a male role model in the home is daunting. Girls need those male arms of love in their life. If they don't have it in their own dad, they will go to great lengths to find it. A girl may make mistake after mistake with men because they are simply begging for a man, any man, to love them. Every girl needs a dad.

What does it do in a boy's life? Statistics show that when a father isn't present, boys are more likely to get in trouble—with the law, with their schools, with anyone in authority. They have not had fathers to put boundaries in their lives. They are more likely to drop out of school before graduation from high school. Families without fathers in the home have a major negative impact on the social and emotional development of children. Boys need the leadership and example of a dad.

Then there's the dad who is there in the home but has no relationship with the children. He barks orders that are to be followed. He doesn't know how to communicate nor relate to his own children. He is either angry or passive. Or take the father who has a favored son to the neglect of another. The wounds go deep in the one who is always looking to please his dad but to no avail. Not a good role model of a father. How tragic in our culture.

There are unimaginable stories of sexual abuse by fathers or other male figures in families. The emotional toll those wounds take is usually very severe. There is also the dad who left the family for another woman, producing scars that last a lifetime.

There are different forms of dysfunction. Unstable parents often create unstable children. A mother may suffer from a mental disorder and that creates an unstable child who is driven to be "normal" at all costs. But the child may emulate the mental illness they have seen on a daily basis.

A child may grow up without a mother or a father who can create stability. Growing up in homes where there is constant strife make a child either like their parent or just the opposite—one who wants peace at any cost or one who is obstinate, mimicking the parent they dislike.

* * *

We are all dysfunctional! Because we live in a fallen world, we are corrupted by sin. We want our way, and when we don't get it, we pout or criticize. And, yes, sibling rivalry is as old as time. We all believe we are the ones who are right. Our siblings, parents, bosses, friends believe they are right. No one is really absolved from the attitude of "my way or the highway." It is ingrained in us from the time we are born to the time we check out of here. Into that backdrop, let's talk about Joseph's family of origin.

Family Dysfunction: The Male Side
Jacob: Father of Joseph

The name *Jacob* means deceiver, manipulator, supplanter, conniver, "*which means one who wrongfully or illegally seizes and holds the place of another*" (Gen. 25:26). Jacob certainly lived up to that name. His name was changed after his encounter with the angel of the Lord. It is my opinion that Jacob knew who the Lord was before this wrestling match with God. His perspective seems to have changed after this encounter. God gave him a new name, Israel, which means "*wrestles with God.*" Henceforth, he would be known by both names.

Will we find out in eternity future that we have a new name, given to us by God at the moment of conversion?

> *He who has an ear, let him hear what the Spirit says to the churches. To him who overcomes, to him I will give some of the hidden manna, and I will give him a white stone, and* a new name *written on the stone which no one knows but he who receives it. (Rev. 2:17)*

As a boy growing up, Jacob's father favored his twin Esau (Gen. 25:28). What did that do in Jacob's life? We know he hung around home with his mother, who favored him. Did she see how Jacob was being treated, so she gave him the attention he craved from his father? We have to read in the white spaces to try to figure this man out. We do know that when a son is wounded by his father and the wounds fester over years of longing to please his dad, it never gets better. Dysfunction is often carried over to the next generation. The sins of the fathers will be manifested in the sons.

> *Then the Lord passed by in front of him and proclaimed, "The Lord, the Lord God, compassionate and gracious, slow to anger, and abounding in lovingkindness and truth; who keeps lovingkindness for thousands, who forgives iniquity, transgression and sin; yet He will by no means leave the guilty unpunished,* visiting the iniquity of fathers on the children and on the grandchildren to the third and fourth generations." (Exod. 34:6)

Was Jacob filled with ingratitude? Did he blame others for his circumstances? Did he blame God? Did he experience love as it was meant to be, or did he love for what it did for him? Jacob, as a deceiver, age sixty, went to work for his uncle Laban (his mother's brother, also a deceiver.) I wonder if that was a characteristic in the family tree? Rebekah and Laban were brother and sister. Did they learn the art of deception from their mom or dad? It would appear so as Rebecca also is a deceiver to her husband and eldest son. She prodded Jacob to deceive his father Isaac for the double blessing of inheritance, always given to the eldest son. It appears that Rebecca had a favorite son! This dysfunction was then carried over to Jacob when we see him favoring two of his sons to the detriment of the other ten.

The Bible never paints a person in a good or righteous light if that's not the case. The Bible is painfully honest when it comes to character traits—good or bad. What does favoritism do in a family already plagued with dishonesty and manipulation? When the sins of the fathers are not dealt with early in life, rebellion and sin are the characteristics he will exhibit later in life. Jacob deceived his father when he was about forty years old. He stole the firstborn blessing from his twin Esau. By the time he was sixty, manipulation and deceit were characteristics firmly entrenched in his life. By the time he turned eighty, well he just couldn't help himself. The whole family experiences the brunt of his warped personality and some of his sons will carry on those same dysfunctions. Only when God intervenes with either a miracle or discipline are those characteristics lessened or alleviated.

It is my opinion that Jacob was an old man (ninety), already set in his ways, when the angel of the Lord appeared to him and wrestled with him. But I get ahead of myself here.

Questions for the Reader

What's the lesson for us? Our parents were not perfect. At times they were anything but easy. Negative characteristics were carried and "taught" to them, either verbally or by watching from their parents. Both blessings and curses go with us through many generations.

What are the negative characteristics given to you by your family of origin? I struggle with anger and a critical spirit. Why? My father was an angry man and very critical. I don't like those characteristics in myself, so I actively pray against and work on not exercising those things. Sometimes it works! Often it doesn't. At times I do act like my dad, to my consternation.

Jacob was sent to his mother's brother to find a wife. He immediately saw his cousin Rachel and was willing to do anything to have her hand in marriage. Laban's contract with Jacob was that he work seven years for Rachel. Was the tradition to marry off the eldest daughter first? Yes. In Genesis 29:26, Laban told Jacob the custom. Did he tell Jacob before he worked seven years? It is my estimation that conversations to that effect *may* have taken place. If Jacob understood, then he deliberately thought Laban wouldn't be so callous as to deceive him.

> *So Jacob served seven years for Rachel and they seemed to him but a few days because of his love for her.*
>
> *Then Jacob said to Laban, "Give me my wife, for my time is completed, that I may go in to her." Laban gathered all the men of the place and made a feast. Now in the evening he took his daughter Leah, and brought her to him; and Jacob went in to her. Laban also gave his maid Zilpah to his daughter Leah as a maid. So it came about in the morning that, behold, it was Leah! And he said to Laban, "What is this you have done to me? Was it not for Rachel that I served with you? Why then have you deceived me?" But Laban said, "It is not the practice in our place to marry off the younger before the firstborn. Complete the week of this one, and we will give you the other also for the service which you shall serve with me for another seven years." Jacob did so and completed her week, and he gave him his daughter Rachel as his wife. Laban also gave his maid Bilhah to his daughter*

*Rachel as her maid. So Jacob went in to Rachel
also, and indeed he loved Rachel more than Leah,
and he served with Laban for another seven years.
(Gen. 29:20–30)*

Laban connived and manipulated with Leah (how far in advance we don't know) but at least on the wedding night he wouldn't let Rachel go to Jacob, instead sent in Leah. It was dark, the sisters probably were equal in size, and Leah was veiled, making the deception logical. Did she speak? Probably not. This was the wedding night, and sex was paramount in Jacob's mind, thinking it was Rachel whom he was sleeping with. After all, he had waited seven years for this wedding night. Nothing could have stopped him from consummating it.

But what he woke up to was Leah instead of Rachel. Talk about being hot under the collar! When he confronted Laban about the "deception," do you think he ever stopped to think about how many times in his own life he used deception to get his way? We never see the sin in our own life, only the sin in someone else's life. How deceived we are!

Then Laban offered Rachel to Jacob within the week, but only if he consented to work another seven years for her. Jacob seethes, but he did it. Do you think the father-in-law relationship was a healthy one? Much deception took place between these two men in the ensuing years. Father-in-law and son-in-law would have a stony cold relationship, deceiving and being deceived by the other until at last they parted. No love lost there!

Sovereignty of God: Does God Overrule Our Decisions?

Let's break in here on the sovereignty of God. Laban was right to offer Leah first. It was tradition. Jacob wasn't about to adhere to tradition or to God's will for that matter. He wanted what he wanted, and he was out to get it, no matter the deception. If Jacob had said yes to Laban and married Leah, I believe he would have been saying yes to God. But stubbornly he was going to get what he wanted. Rachel was his driving force.

You see, *Leah was the "chosen" one* for Jacob *by God*. It was she who would belong in the lineage of the Messiah, the most prominent theology of the Old Testament. From Genesis 3 forward the way was made for the redemption of the Messiah, the Son of God, who would take away the sins of the world. God deliberately weeded out other tribes and concentrated on the tribe that would carry on the plan of redemption. We see that when God chose the lineage of Messiah in the early part of Genesis: Adam, Seth, Noah. He then narrowed the lineage to Shem, Abraham, Isaac, and Jacob. It's interesting to note that we don't know the names of some of the wives in early Genesis (Noah, Shem, etc), but now we are going to know the names of the wives in the lineage. Abraham and Sarah (not Hagar), Isaac and Rebekah, Jacob and Leah (not Rachel).

Because Jacob had an incredibly stubborn streak in him, he wasn't in tune with God and his will for his life. He was a very selfish man who was out to please number one. God needed to break him. Would it now be through gaining the chosen wife from God? Would Jacob bow the knee and say to God, "Whatever you want for me is what I want." Instead he dug his heels in deeper and worked another seven years to gain the coveted woman of his choice.

Jacob never gave that thought room to work in his life. Had he accepted God's will for his life, he would have grown to love Leah. He never did.

Jacob never asked God whom he should marry. Instead he chose a wife whom God had not chosen. Now there was nothing wrong with being attracted to Rachel. But had he stopped and asked God for His will, God would have shown him clearly that he was to marry Leah. Jacob never looked under the surface of a pretty face to the heart of Leah. If he had, he would have seen in her a heart that was pliable. But he didn't. He couldn't see past his own desires.

Later, when meeting up with his brother Esau (Gen. 31), he paid lip service to being happy to see his twin. But that was short lived as he deceived him again and went on his way with his wealth. I am sure there was not a lot of love lost between these brothers. Anyone who plays deception games with people never wins in the end. Yes, Jacob was a patriarch but not a very good character to emulate. The Bible paints Jacob in a negative light, even though he is in the Messianic lineage. His acts of faith are few. In Hebrews 11, Jacob is mentioned but it's at the end of his life when he blesses his sons and through that blessing predicts their future.

Did God choose Jacob? Yes. But he is not considered a man of faith. He had an if-then kind of attitude toward God. "If You…then I will serve You" (Gen. 28:20). I love God's patience in taking us right where we are in our faith journey. Jacob didn't have a personal relationship with God until God brought him to Bethel and confronted Jacob in a most direct way.

How many times in our life have we gone ahead of God? We don't pray. We don't seek God's face or His will. We just simply do what we want to do, when we want to do it. And we suffer the consequences sometimes for the rest of our lives. We are like the people in the book of Judges who do "what is right in their own eyes," never consulting the One who made us and knows what's best for us. We selfishly go on our way, hoping for the best to work out. Usually God is pursuing us, and we either aren't listening, or we are deliberately doing what we want in the face of Almighty God. We have all been there.

Getting Jacob's Attention

So now how was God going to get Jacob's attention? He now had two wives—one whom he loved and one who was just there when he needed sex and sons. He was still the selfish stubborn man who had no idea of a relationship with the Almighty God. Oh, he knew there was a God. He sort of believed in Him. He had been taught that from his father Isaac. He saw Isaac's devotion. But somehow it had never crossed his mind that he too needed a personal relationship with this awesome Power. I think he didn't even care to know this unseen God. All he was after was what made him happy. And even that was elusive!

Jacob was probably ninety years old by this time. He had lived his whole life deceiving and being deceived. Was he difficult to live with? A person who by nature tries to mislead, manipulate, lie, and underestimate everyone else is miserable. Can anyone ever trust him? Can he even trust himself?

He had eleven sons by this time but even that didn't satisfy him, He was still self-absorbed. Rachel had been barren, and he ached for her to bear his children. Rachel was barren for twenty years before getting pregnant with her firstborn. Joseph means "taken away my reproach" (Gen. 30:23). At least she bore him one son. Did it make him happy? For a time, yes. But he was still a miserable man. There was a hole in his heart, and he didn't know how to fix it. He had always been able to fix things by manipulation, but now he couldn't.

God said, "Okay, Jacob. I haven't been able to get your attention throughout your life. You have stolen, manipulated, deceived your father, your twin brother, your uncle and all his servants. You think you have manipulated Me. Think again. I am not a man that you can ignore me. You cannot manipulate me. You cannot lie and cheat me. I now have to break you if you cannot and won't submit to my leading in your life." And that's what God did.

After leaving Laban, traveling with his four wives and eleven sons, God came in the middle of the night in the form of an angel (Jesus Christ in the OT came often as the angel of the Lord) and began a wrestling match with him.

Now he arose that same night and took his two wives and his two maids and his eleven children, and crossed the ford of the Jabbok. He took them and sent them across the stream. And he sent across whatever he had. Then Jacob was left alone, and a man wrestled with him until daybreak. When he saw that he had not prevailed against him, he touched the socket of his thigh; so the socket of Jacob's thigh was dislocated while he wrestled with him. Then he said, "Let me go, for the dawn is breaking." But he said, "I will not let you go unless you bless me." So he said to him, "What is your name?" And he said, "Jacob." He said, "Your name shall no longer be Jacob, but Israel; for you have striven with God and with men and have prevailed." Then Jacob asked him and said, "Please tell me your name." But he said, "Why is it that you ask my name?" And he blessed him there. So Jacob named the place Peniel, for he said, "I have seen God face to face, yet my life has been preserved." Now the sun rose upon him just as he crossed over Penuel, and he was limping on his thigh. (Gen. 32:22–31)

What is it like to be in the ring with God and be sucker punched by Him? Jacob wrestled until the pain in his thigh put him flat on his face to the ground. Ask any doctor and he will tell you the sinew of the thigh is the strongest part of the human body. When it is injured, it's one of the most excruciating pains you can feel. God got his attention! Jacob said, "I have wrestled with God and survived! God was the One who won that wrestling match. He will always win because He knows what is best for us at all times. Sometimes He saves us from the very characteristics in our life that take us down a slippery slope. And when God can't get our attention, He will go for the most painful place in us. For most of us it's our hearts that get wounded.

At that point Jacob stopped wrestling and submitted for the first time in his life, and he was an old man! We don't know the full conversation, only that the wrestling match took place. (Gen. 32:28). We also know that Jacob was humbled by this experience. Jacob knew that it was God who had done this. And God knew he now had Jacob's attention.

After Jacob wrestled with the angel of the Lord, he came away with a different attitude and instructed his family members to put away their foreign gods. He had a change of heart, albeit a small one. Was there life change? As much as was possible with an old man set in his ways. God knew that Jacob had come to the end of himself and so changed his name from Jacob (manipulator) to *Israel*, "one who wrestles or strives with God." *El* in a name always says "God." *Isra* means "strives or wrestles." Other books say the name means "prince of God." I am going to choose the former definition. Jacob wrestled with God and survived! How often do we wrestle with God over some issue or some person? I like to think that *we are all Israel*, wrestling with God numerous times in our lives when we don't understand what is going on or when we need clear direction.

Small Changes

How was Jacob changed after that? He still had a habit of lying (we will encounter this trait later in the story of Joseph). He still didn't know how to tell the whole truth. He had prejudice toward the boys of Rachel. So what was changed? He believed in God. He knew He existed. He knew his life was in the hands of the Almighty. God had proven Himself faithful to Jacob. Is there ever radical change in us? When we become believers, we have a new spirit within us but we are still the same people. We struggle with many of the same issues. Most of our lives we have to trust God for issues that seem never to change. Changes in life come as we are more quickly convicted of our sinful ways, learning little by little to submit to the powerful hand of the Almighty. The earlier one becomes a believer, the more life change takes place. The later-in-life change seems to inch along slowly. We have too many habits that need changing. Some change dramatically, while others take more time.

Statistics on Age of Belief

Age matters when it comes to salvation. The younger we are when we become a believer, the better for the humbling process in life. Becoming a Christian as a child gives God more time for the maturation process. Teens have seen enough sin in their lives to begin that process of softening as well. However, when a person becomes a Christian as an adult, and especially as an older adult, the changes can sometimes be minimal. My own father became a Christian in his fifties. The changes were minute although I was assured that he understood salvation. His language didn't stop altogether, he just dropped a few words. He read the Bible a little bit more, but never devoured it. Because I began to tell him I loved him, he too started using the words "I love you too." But he was never an initiator of that phrase. Small changes, but enough for me to know it was real.

Statistics show that the earlier a child comes to Christ is the best chance of breaking some of the dysfunction in the child. Changes take time, prayer, effort, and a whole lot of trust in Almighty God.

* * *

Statistics presented by George Barna in the book titled, *Evangelism Is Most Effective among Kids* (2009):

- Before the age of 18 is our best chance of becoming Christians.
- 9 out of 10 conversions take place by high school age.
- After age 18 conversions decrease dramatically.
- Ages 25–35: 1 in 5,000 will receive Christ
- Ages 36–45: 1 in 25,000
- Over 46 years: 1 in 80,000

Current Barna statistics:

- 43 percent of all Americans who accept Jesus Christ as their savior do so before age thirteen.
- 64 percent made that commitment to Christ before their eighteenth birthday.
- 13 percent made their profession of faith while eighteen to twenty-one years old.
- 23 percent embraced Christ after their twenty-first birthday.

Barna noted that these figures are consistent with similar studies it has conducted during the past twenty years.

The survey data show that Catholics who become born again are even more likely than Protestants to do so before reaching high school. Among those currently associated with a Catholic church and who are born again, two out of three (66 percent) accepted Christ before age thirteen, one-fifth (21 percent) did so from thirteen to twenty-one, and the remaining 13 percent made that decision as an adult. In contrast, born again people aligned with a Protestant church make that choice at an older age: 40 percent did so as children, 35 percent during the 13 to 21 age span, and one-quarter (25 percent) as adults.

People who become Christians before their teen years are more likely than those who are converted when older to remain "absolutely committed" to Christianity. However, they are also less likely to believe that a profession of faith in Jesus Christ is the only way to get to heaven and they are less prone to watch Christian television. While they are just as likely as other believers to share their faith in Christ with non-Christians, they are less likely to do so through exploratory dialogue with their friends.

* * *

If these statistics are correct, then we must teach and train our children while they are still young to follow the Lord. We must teach them how to make their walk with the Lord personal at every age. The definition of spiritual growth is this: "*The life of Jesus produced in us by the power of the Holy Spirit, according to the Word of God, invading every area of human life.*" Our children need our example, our teaching, our discipline, yes; but more than that, they need Jesus in them, working the work that only the Holy Spirit can produce for a lifetime of fruitful living.

Are you like Jacob? Sometimes I feel I still am. I would love to be more like the man this book is about. But sometimes don't we just want to give up because of the Jacob characteristics in our lives? We still get angry. We still have petty jealousies. We still don't think life is fair. We think we are in control of our lives, and if life doesn't go as planned, we are disappointed. Sometimes we resort to making "deals" with God: "If You do this, I will do that."

I don't know what your issues are, but I do know what mine are. I think as we grow in the Lord we are quicker to see God, quicker to see His hand in His dealings with us. But still when we get wounded by someone, we have the human reaction of wanting to "get back" and do harm to that person. We can change as we see the good hand of God in our circumstances, but change takes time to process.

What are your besetting sins that never seem to change or go away? We all have them and have our lifetime to deal with them. Maturity is not getting rid of those things in our lives, but it is seeing quicker and quicker the folly of our ways and that those besetting sins really don't help us much especially in the necessity of the maturation process.

Notice in the Bible that God took Joseph out of his dysfunctional family at age seventeen. That was an appropriate age at which God worked to produce in him the man that he eventually would become. It was mandatory that he leave his family and go through a series of tests to know what was in his heart. Notice the Deuteronomy passage below. This is what God does in our lives when He takes us through trials. It doesn't matter what era of time you live in—Old Testament times, New Testament times, or present time. The process is the same. Various trials test our obedience to the known Word of God. God humbles us and tests us so that He will know what is in our hearts. He did it then; He does it now.

> *You shall* remember *all the way which the Lord your God has led you in the wilderness these forty years, that He might* humble you, testing you, to know what was in your heart, *whether you would keep His commandments or not.* He humbled you *and let you be hungry, and fed you with manna which you did not know, nor did your fathers know, that He might make you understand that man does not live by bread alone, but man lives by everything that proceeds out of the mouth of the Lord. (Deut. 8:2–3)*

God took Joseph from his family of origin because of the sinful traits of his father and also of his brothers. God needed a clean slate on which to write on his heart. Joseph's young age was a benefit to him. God would take this young man and groom him to make him a man of faith. This process would take time. He would be taken to a different culture, with different laws, a different language. He would need to learn to lean heavily on a God these people knew nothing about. He would have to rely on what he knew from his family of origin, but he would have to learn there was oh so much more to this God whom he thought he knew.

Keep in mind as we look at the next chapter that names are significant in telling stories. We will encounter the actual testimony of one mother as we look into the female side. We will encounter another testimony from a father later in the book about Joseph. Names were laden with meaning. This will never be so evident as it is when discussing the stepmothers of Joseph. Each one had a story to tell, but we will look at Leah specifically.

Questions for Chapter 1:

1)   Share some of the dysfunction in your family from your
     father's side.

2)   How has this dysfunction tested your faith or motivated
     you to change?

3)   What did God do in your life after you left home at age
     _____?

CHAPTER 2

DYSFUNCTIONAL FAMILIES: FEMALE SIDE

The Four Mothers of Joseph

We will experience some uncomfortable moments looking at this dysfunctional family. We will wonder how Joseph ever came out of this family unscathed. But I digress, and I believe God in his sovereignty took him out of this family to teach him what He couldn't teach him inside the family compound. Here's his backstory:

Jacob worked seven years for the love of his life, Rachel. Instead he married Leah and then one week later, Rachel. He worked fourteen years for his father-in-law for these two wives. Rachel he loved. Leah, he did not. What did this do to Leah? Let's find out.

Obviously Jacob was intimate with both wives. One of them got pregnant; the other did not. Can you guess which one? Yes, Leah. She was so excited that now she would be a mother. In that culture, having children, especially sons, was a sign of favor from God and favor with her husband. So during the many months of pregnancy she knew she was the favored one and how that must have galled her pretty younger sister. She knew Jacob loved Rachel. Now love was a possibility for her as well. In times past, having children gave a woman status.

Ah, to love and be loved. *Leah* (meaning weary, delicate) longed to be loved. Her dreams were tied to the hope that her husband, Jacob, would grow to love her.

> *Now the Lord saw that Leah was unloved, and He opened her womb, but Rachel was barren. Leah conceived and bore a son and named him Reuben, for she said, "Because the Lord has seen my afflic-tion;* surely now my husband will love me." *Then she conceived again and bore a son and said, "Because the Lord has heard that* I *am unloved, He has therefore given me this son also." So she named him Simeon. She conceived again and bore a son and said, "Now this time my husband will* become attached to me, *because I have borne him three sons." Therefore he was named Levi. (Gen. 29:31–34)*

Do you see her story unfolding with the names of her sons? When Leah became pregnant with her first son, she hoped it would change her circumstances. Names in the Old Testament were often given to *signify what was happening in the life of a parent.* Listen to her heart as she names her sons.

Reuben, her firstborn, meant *"surely now my husband will love me."* Leah obviously pinned her hopes on this son. Did Jacob notice her anymore? No, he still loved Rachael and demonstrated it every time he saw her. But at night he would slip into Leah's tent, make love to her, and hurry out to Rachael the following day. Well, she had a son. She would pour her love into him and maybe someday her husband would love her too.

Leah's unrequited longing continued with the birth of Simeon, which meant, "*I am unloved.*" Wow, she admitted that having sons for this man didn't mean love. It simply meant sex and status.

When she got pregnant with the third son, she named him Levi, stating, "*Now my husband will become attached to me.*" The word *attached* is a far cry from love. Love was out of the question. Now, if he would just acknowledge her, she would be happy. To her shattered dreams and agonizing prayers, the silence of God seemed deafening. Would this man, whom she was married to, ever love her? Would he ever acknowledge her presence? Would he acknowledge her ability to give him sons? Notice, love was not even a prayer anymore. She just longed to be noticed.

She was a slave of fear—the fear of never hearing the words "I love you." She was bound and gagged by fear. She had questions that were left unanswered. She longed for fulfillment, not just of children but of love from her husband. After the birth of each son, Jacob went right on with life as if nothing had happened. She had sons. Shouldn't that be enough? She knew she wasn't special, far from it. She was drowning in a whirlwind of fear. Her tears were dry. There were no words. The garment of depression shrouded her very being. Could anything lift her countenance?

The Leah Factor: Discovering the Love of God

As she lay in her tent, night after night, something mysterious began to take place in the depth of her soul. No more looking at Jacob as a god in her life. "I may never be the loved wife I always dreamed of. It's okay! It's not about me, or my husband, or my sons. It's all about God."

And she conceived again and bore a son and said, "This time I will praise the Lord." *Therefore she named him Judah. Then she stopped bearing.* (Gen. 29:35)

With the birth of her fourth son, the name upon her lips was "Judah," *"this time I will praise the Lord."* The Hound of Heaven broke through, and she broke free. She stopped wrestling. No more crawling in the dust. "This time I *choose* praise." She was no longer a slave of fear. She became a child of God. What a powerful testimony Leah has left for us.

God finally had her attention and her heart. She knew God's love for her was unshakable, everlasting. Leah could now rejoice, even though her circumstances remained unchanged. She could now be full of praise and thanksgiving because it was to God she was looking to meet her needs. She had been looking in the wrong direction, to a man to meet her longing for love. Her focus became the great God of the universe. I call this "the Leah factor." A life change occurred, not because of who she was, but because she found out who God was to her. Could this have been her "conversion" moment when she entered a life of faith? I believe it was.

Application to Us

I don't know how many times in my years of counseling women in their marriages I have had to say, "I don't know if this will ever change, but your longing must be for your Heavenly Father and not your earthly husband. Go into your prayer closet and pray. And don't give up." So often it's when we pray, sometimes for years, that Yahweh shows up and reveals what it has been about all along. It's about us getting our hearts right with our Creator and stop expecting people to meet our needs. Someone once said, *"The killer of relationships is expectations.*" This was true of Leah. It is also true of us. God wants our hearts first and foremost.

If you've been hurt by someone you loved, you've played the if-onlys and what-ifs a thousand times to no avail. You may be in a marriage without the love you desired. Your marriage may have already failed. But God is not through with you.

God is relentless in His pursuit of you until you give it all up to Him—your dreams, your hopes, your desires. He may have allowed great pain in your life to bring you to this place. Only at His feet is He free to give you what you most long for. The key that unlocked the door to Leah's heart was submission to the Hound of Heaven. The result was praise on her lips and in her life. If you identify with Leah, you might want to express it to the Lord.

Lord, at times I feel so unloved. I feel trapped in a loveless marriage. But through Leah's example, I am choosing this day to praise You. Thank you for loving me with true, unconditional, and everlasting love. You have a plan for me that's beyond my comprehension. I trust You with my life and the circumstances that seem beyond my control. My life is yours, now and forever. Do with me as You choose. Lead me where you want me to go. Make of me the woman I long to be. Amen

I am anxious to meet this amazing woman someday. I believe her conversion to God came with the birth of Judah. She had been the ugly sister all her life. People had always paid attention to her younger more beautiful sister. Rachel was cuter. She was funnier. She garnered the attention of others. Have you been there?

Maybe *you* are the younger (or older), prettier sister and you have watched as people have paid great attention to you. What has that done to your sibling? And more so, what has it done to you? Have you ignored your sibling, or friend, or family member because you were favored? Have you had compassion for others who are less successful, less beautiful? You may need to ask God how to deal with those whom you hurt or ignored. Does God want you to reach out and touch them in ways they need?

Conversion is a strange thing. For some, hearing a message on the love of God is what pulled them toward Him. For others, it may be a gradual realization that no matter what you do, salvation is unreachable without direct intervention from God. I look at the people of the Old Testament and ask the question, how did God break through to their hearts? We saw that with Jacob when God wrestled with him and wounded him deeply. We see it here as Leah wrestled with God over being unloved by her husband.

With Leah it was unrequited and unfulfilled longing for love. It was really the love that only God could give. God gave her gifts of sons, but what she really needed was the gift of His love. She saw that and believed. Her life was never the same after that. When we meet people in heaven I believe we will want to hear more of their story. I want to talk with Leah. I want to hear her heart. I want to sit at her feet. A wounded believer has a powerful testimony. She, who was deeply wounded, became a woman of praise. Judah (praise)! What a wonderful reminder of Who God is to us.

God honored her in life and in death. She was buried in the cave of Machpelah with Jacob and the other patriarchs: Abraham and Sarah, Isaac and Rebecca, and Jacob and Leah. Their tombs have been visited by millions of people throughout history in the town of Hebron in Israel. God has a way of redeeming, not only in this life but in the life to come. Our stories go with us into eternity. The pain of our stories will be gone. Perspective will take us by surprise. It's been said that the most often used word in heaven will be "Oh!"

Rachel

Leah's sister, *Rachel* (meaning "ewe"), finally conceived after twenty years of marriage and had a son whom she named Joseph (meaning increaser, addition, taken away reproach). Her longing was not for love but for children. Rachel did a crazy thing before God gave her a child of her own. She asked Jacob to sleep with her maid in order to give Rachel a child through her, a surrogate (Sarah and Hagar?). Then Leah used the same tactic. Rachel conceived, and then Leah conceived again and again. What a family dynamic! Habits die hard when there is jealousy and unfulfilled dreams on all sides. Can you see the young boys as they were growing up, watching this tug-of-war on Jacob? These women whose only hope was having children by Jacob?

Even though Leah had a change of heart, she was still married to Jacob for the rest of her life. She did bear him other children. I don't believe though that her longing was for Jacob. She simply did what was required of her, and she bore him other children. Her hope had to be placed in her God who never let her down. Every time she spoke Judah's name and kissed his cheeks, God reminded her. We may have a change in a moment's conversion, but there will never come a time when we don't need reminding that it's God we need, God who fulfills, and God that cares.

The rest of the book will be about Rachael's son Joseph. We don't have much information on Rachel. We don't see as much of her story in the naming of her two sons but we have enough. Joseph means "taken away my reproach," and her second son, Benjamin, which means "son of my sorrow" because with his birth she knew she was dying. So her story was one of longing to be pregnant and give Jacob children. After twenty long years of waiting, her reproach had been taken away. By this time, however, she was too old to be bearing children and pregnancy and childbirth was difficult for her. With her second and last pregnancy, she knew her health was failing. She probably prayed long and hard that the child in her womb would survive her failing body.

Death followed the difficult birth of Benjamin. What a pain-filled life she also had. For twenty years she watched the women around her conceive and give her husband sons. How difficult. With those exciting moments in the life of Jacob, hers were only tears. Yes, her story indeed is in the names she gave her sons. Can't you feel her sorrow? Can you see her depression? And Leah saw it too. She wasn't a callous woman. This after all, was her younger sister whom she still loved, even though jealousy was a part of their family dynamic.

Do you see the dysfunction of these two women? One desired love because it was unattainable. The other desired children, and that too was unattainable. We all have a longing for something deep within our souls. As God reveals that to us, we must put those longings clearly at His feet for Him to do with us as He chooses. Our desires may never be fulfilled in this lifetime. But God wants to be to us all we need. As human beings, we want our own glory, our own recognition of why we matter. When we begin to realize that it's not about us, it's about Him, it's about His glory. At that point we have a change of heart. Peace replaces turmoil. Courage replaces fear. Satisfaction replaces bitterness.

The Sovereignty of the Almighty

Let me throw another curve ball here. If we believe that in this puzzle of the Old Testament there is a sovereign plan, let's see what is given here. Remember, the top of the box of this puzzle is the Messianic lineage. It goes from Adam to Jesus in an unbroken line: Adam to Noah, Shem to Judah. Then it narrows from Judah through David to Jesus in the New Testament. We now understand DNA, but from God's viewpoint, the DNA was always in play in the Messianic lineage. God narrows from broad to ever increasing detail as the New Testament emerges in history.

Since we are studying the family of Jacob, let me ask a question here. Whose DNA is combined with that of Jacob to produce the lineage? Leah! And it's interesting always that it isn't the firstborn son, it's the fourth son, in whom the lineage will take place. Jacob is unaware of God's sovereignty, as is Leah. But God is fully aware of what He is doing. Isaiah 14:24 says, "*Surely, just as I have intended so it has happened, and just as I have planned, so it will stand.*"

You see, *Jacob* had *to marry Leah*. He didn't want to. Laban deceived him. But God had led him to this family. Jacob chose Rachel, but *God chose Leah*. Even though the marriage didn't take place in Jacob's plan of schemes, it took place because the Lord of the universe planned it so.

God's sovereign plan and purposes will be accomplished, and no human or demonic opposition can thwart them. His plan will go forward unabated. No matter the circumstances. No matter the desire of the people involved. God was behind Jacob's move to Laban's homestead. Setbacks, opposition, and disappointments will not alter God's purposes for Leah or for Jacob. The same holds true for my life and yours.

Parents have long had influence over their children. That influence can be good and bad. But God's purposes for us will win in the end. We cannot thwart them. We cannot change them. We cannot manipulate a God who knows and sees and leads and determines.

Throughout the Old Testament God's sovereign will comes through. The Messiah would come through His choice of people. It would be second-born Shem, not Japeth or Ham.

God told Abram that he would have a child and that through that child would come the Redeemer. Sarah understood the prophecy, but time marched on, and it just didn't happen. So she took the prophecy into her own hands and asked Abram to have a son for her from Hagar. Of course, Abram complies (what man wouldn't?). But God said no, not Hagar, but Sarah. Ishmael was Abram's firstborn. But God had chosen another, the firstborn of Abram and Sarah. In other words, the second born.

Isaac and Rebecca had twin sons: Esau born first; Jacob, second. It is through Jacob that Messiah will come. Jacob and Leah had three sons, but it is through the fourth son that Messiah would come. God is on the throne. His plans will prevail, no matter the era of time or the people whom God will use to fulfill that plan.

Now does that mean that God didn't love Rachel? No, He loved her always. But she was a "peeling," as will be her sons. But God still has a purpose for those who are not of his Messianic lineage. Joseph will show us just how important each and every one of us is to the plan and purpose of God. "God loves us and has a plan for our lives." How many times have you heard that? Do you believe it?

Let me interject a very important scripture here on Jacob, his ancestry, and his lineage. We must never forget that God does not see as we do, nor does He evaluate life as we do, not does He choose as we do.

> *The Lord did not set His love on you nor choose you because you were more in number than any of the peoples, for you were the fewest of all peoples, but because the Lord loved you and kept the oath which He swore to your forefathers, the Lord brought you out by a mighty hand and redeemed you from the house of slavery, from the hand of Pharaoh king of Egypt. Know therefore that the Lord your God, He is God, the faithful God, who keeps His covenant and His lovingkindness to a thousandth generation with those who love Him and keep His commandments. (Deut. 7:7–9)*

Review:

Keep in mind the two-pronged purpose of the Old Testament Scriptures:

The Messianic Lineage: from Adam to Abraham to David to Jesus

Detailed Messianic Genealogy in Old Testament: 1 Chronicles 1–3

New Testament Genealogy of Jesus:
Matthew and Luke begin with those same genealogies:
Matthew, speaking to the Jews, begins with Abraham to Jesus.
Luke, speaking to all humanity, begins with Adam to Jesus.
The Faith Line is depicted in Hebrews 11.

Questions for Chapter 2

1) What are the dysfunctions of your mother's side of the family tree?

2) What are the good traits that have been passed to you?

3) What are your children's names, and how did you come up with them?

4) In what ways do you see the sovereign hand of God on your life?

CHAPTER 3

WOUNDED PEOPLE
WOUND PEOPLE

Jacob had a favored wife, so are we surprised that he now has a favored son!

A Wounded Band of Brothers

> *His brothers saw that their father loved him more than all his brothers; and so they hated him and could not speak to him on friendly terms. (Gen. 37:4)*

Jacob had ten sons by three women before Rachel's first pregnancy. They had waited twenty long years for this sought-after child, and now he was here. Jacob made no bones about his favoritism. Isn't it interesting that Jacob already had a child who would be the pre-runner to the Messiah? Judah had already been born, but to Jacob he was equal with all his brothers. God was going to single him out in the blessings Jacob would eventually give all his sons at his death, recorded in the last chapters of Genesis. But not yet.

When Rachel found that she was pregnant, both she and Jacob were ecstatic. Jacob, now an old man (around age eighty-seven) had loved this woman all her life and favored her above his other wives. Even though Leah had given him sons and a daughter and both of the maids had each given him sons, it was to Rachel whom he poured affection. So, humanly speaking, Joseph was showered with love and affection and gifts from the time he was born. The other sons watched with amazement and bewilderment at the lavish affection Joseph received.

Joseph was the eleventh son. This kid could do no wrong in the eyes of his father or his mother. What happens in a child's life when the parents are prejudiced toward him from his birth? Not only did his father and mother treat him special, the other mothers and their sons watched as day after day, month after month, year after year, Joseph was treated differently. Can't you hear the conversations around their dinner tables? The whole clan hated what was so obnoxiously obvious.

Rachel's death came with the birth of a younger brother to Joseph, Benjamin, meaning "son of my sorrow." Benjamin was the youngest son of Jacob and always stayed close to his father. With Rachel gone, Jacob placed his affection (very obvious and blatant) upon Joseph and Benjamin. They could do no wrong.

These are the records of the generations of Jacob. Joseph, when seventeen years of age, was pasturing the flock with his brothers (through Leah) while he was still a youth, along with the sons of Bilhah and the sons of Zilpah, his father's wives. And Joseph brought back a bad report about them to their father. Now Israel loved Joseph more than all his sons, because he was the son of his old age; and he made him a varicolored tunic. His broth-

ers saw that their father loved him more than all his brothers; and so they hated him and could not speak to him on friendly terms. (Gen. 37:2-4)

The story of Joseph really began taking on momentum when Joseph turned into a teen/adult. Joseph was seventeen years old, and Jacob lavished him with a prized possession. To dye goat hair or wool into different colors would have taken time and skill to produce. Clothing made from animal skin was easy, but it was always a dull beige or brown. So plants were used in the dyeing process. It says that Jacob gave Joseph a coat of "many" colors. That would have taken time to produce the different colors and then weave them into a type of throw/cloak.

When their father blatantly showered affection on Joseph, the ten older brothers became incensed. That was the last straw. After all, they were sons of Jacob as well. Why did Joseph get everything? They had to work. They had to tend sheep. They never got a special garment or any other gift. What right did Joseph have? I am sure this was not the first time Joseph had been favored before his brothers. It would be like Christmas—where only one son would get a gift. The others were completely left out. The gift wasn't a secret. It was there for all of them to see. What was Jacob thinking? Obviously Jacob was a wounded and selfish soul, which made him a callous, hardened, manipulative, insensitive man, wounding others without thought.

What happens in a family when one child is viewed as a favorite in front of all the rest? Not good feelings toward that child! I am sure they all struggled with their dad too, but the brother— that was who they hated. They made no bones about it all Joseph's life. But this took the cake. Now he was coming to meet them in their place of work, and he was showing off his coat! How dare he! Sounds to me that he was a spoiled brat. I am sure that not only did the ten brothers have a problem with him, but probably all three remaining mothers did too: Leah, Bilah, and Zilpah.

Years of wounding for these ten brothers by their dad was now going to take its toll. It's a logical part of the brain that says, "Hey, am I not worthy of your love? If so, why don't you do for me what you do for him?" Woundedness creates a "me" life. It's all about me. What did I do? What can I do? Why did he/she say that? Why did they do that? When we are in the "it's all about me" stage, nothing good can come of it. Every human being has been wounded by someone. There are no exceptions. People say things in anger. Oh, they apologize, but they shouldn't have said it in the first place. We want to crawl into our hole of protectiveness and hope it all goes away. But it never does. Isn't woundedness the story of us all?

When we are wounded, we tend to think of our own needs. Self cannot look out for others. We also don't see that when we get our feelings hurt and don't try to understand the other person, we concentrate on self even more. How am I feeling as opposed to how someone else feels? We also tend to feel our own pain to the exclusion of the other person's pain. We feel we have been "more hurt" and that the other person is insensitive to our needs. We ask the question, "Why does he/she hurt me every time I see them?" When this scenario happens, the next time we encounter that person, the hurt piles on top of the last hurt. I don't want to minimize how people wound us. I am saying that when we are wounded, it tends to be all about us. Our pain may be so severe we can hardly breathe. That kind of pain is excruciating, and I will deal with that in a later chapter. Pain is real, and it hurts!

Understanding Teens

Joseph's brothers were considerably older than he was. Some were married and had begun their own families. Reuben was twenty years older than Joseph, so he was thirty-seven. Given close birth years for some these ten brothers, half would have been in the thirties and the other half in the twenties. All were working men, shepherding sheep. Joseph was a teenager. Do seventeen-year-olds have great discernment? No, they do not. To boot, he came to tell them about a couple dreams he had. Wow, how to rub salt in a wound! They already hated this kid. Now here he is with his beautiful new coat swaying in the breeze and prideful words oozing out of his mouth. It was more than they could stomach.

I have four children, a son who is oldest and then three daughters. Todd was a rule follower, a good kid, and a leader among his peers. Don and I watched as he started to become a man. But sometimes he would argue with me or tell me he had a better idea. Sometimes it sounded like disrespect to me and to Don, who always corrected Todd with, "You will not talk to your mother like that," to which Todd would back down. But he was beginning to cut the apron strings in thinking for himself and making that known to us. When Todd was seventeen, I found a sign that read, *"Hire a teenager while he still knows everything."* I lovingly put that in the kitchen and told him that the sign was for him. The sign stayed there till Todd's junior year in college when I didn't feel it was appropriate anymore. Todd had learned how to better express himself as he matured.

Teens don't really know how to express their growing adult feelings to their parents. They certainly don't know how to do that with their siblings. This is where Joseph was at the time. No discernment on any count. His brothers were older and had passed the immaturity of the teen years. Now they had to put up with him. If you have ever had teens in your home, you know what it's like. Those are not bad years. In fact, those years happened to be my favorite age for all four kids. I loved watching them become adults and begin to think like adults. The teen years, however, are probably the most selfish time in a person's life. Everything revolves around them—their friends, their fun, their thoughts. It's all about them. It's okay because we've all been there. I can remember my own father saying to me during my teen years, "You think you know everything!" I hate to admit it, but I did think that!

I once asked my mother how she stood me as a teen. I remember those wild swings of moods and throwing things and flying off the handle and, yes, sassing my parents. I thought my mom would say something like, "Oh, it wasn't so bad." But what she said stunned me: "It was really hard. I never knew what mood I would find you in." Of course, I didn't think I was *that* bad, but Mom did!

Teens can be sassy, sarcastic, volatile, and moody. They always have one person in mind: themselves. It is a "me-mine" stage. They are up one day and down the next. You want to see another mood, wait five minutes. Hormones and bodies are changing by the hour. That's why parents often dread the teen years. Instead of dreading them, understand them, flow with them, and one day they will surprise you at how mature they really are. Teens are the last to understand what is going on in their growing bodies. By the time they reach the twenties much of those moods have settled down and they begin to settle into who they are. We must all pass into adulthood the same way—through the door of the teen years.

The teen years are not all bad. But we must understand that teens are in the transition from a childhood to becoming an adult and so emotions swing, sometimes wildly. Teens are beginning to want to know who they are and what they will become one day. For some they are natural leaders and create a small following of their peers. For some, they are followers and try as much as possible to go along with the crowd. In the Song of Solomon chapter 8, it talks about teens as walls or doors when it comes to the sexual arena. I watched and prayed for each of my teens that they would be walls and not doors that could easily swing with each passing temptation. A wall stays strong in terms of temptations and leads rather than follows. Every personality has a tendency to go one way or the other. We shall see that in Joseph's life as well.

Let's look at some statistics here on teenagers and their brains. "The rational part of a teen's brain isn't fully developed and won't be until he or she is *twenty-five years old* or so. In fact, recent research has found that adult and teen brains work differently. Adults think with the prefrontal cortex, the brain's rational part."[1]

Children who get into addictions (pornography, drugs, alcohol, sex) when they are between eleven to thirteen years old and continue that behavior will have more tendency to have lifelong addictions. Before the late teen years, judgment is lacking in the brain to fully understand what is going on. Teens can be too trusting of the opposite sex, which can land them in trouble.

Becoming addicted is typically a gradual process and involves many distinct but interdependent factors, including the timing of various experiences.

Research clearly shows that most adults with addictions first developed these problems during adolescence or young adulthood. This finding makes sense from a developmental perspective, since teenagers have greater access to alcohol, drugs, and other potentially addictive experiences as they gain more independence from their parents. From a biological perspective, adolescence is a time in which the parts of the brain responsible for impulsivity, decision-making, and executive control are undergoing considerable change and are not yet fully mature. Exposure to experiences that can alter brain architecture in these same areas may increase the likelihood of developing an addiction.[2]

---

[1]   ("Understanding the Teen Brain," Health Encyclopedia, University of Rochester Medical Center)

[2]   ("Understanding the Teen Brain," Health Encyclopedia, University of Rochester Medical Center https://www.urmc.rochester.edu/.../c... University of Rochester Medical Center)

Remember at this time, Joseph was a typical teenager. His judgment was faulty concerning his father, his mother, and his brothers. He hadn't thought through his dreams, nor the way he was treated differently from the rest of the siblings. He had *no* discernment.

This kid had the audacity to flaunt his coat and then to brag about his incredible dreams. This would be like having ten older siblings who stayed close to home to tend to their father's business. Then here comes the eleventh sibling and says he's going to become "somebody" while they remained "nobody." He would be afforded opportunity that the others would not. That's what his dreams seemed like to them. Here are the dreams. Not one of the brothers asked what the dreams meant. All they heard was that Joseph would be elevated above them. Listen as he tells them the details. Listen to his tone of voice and his audacity to brag.

Joseph's Dreams

Then Joseph had a dream, and when he told it to his brothers, they hated him even more. *He said to them, "Please listen to this dream which I have had; or behold, we were binding sheaves in the field, and lo, my sheaf rose up and also stood erect; and behold, your sheaves gathered around and bowed down to my sheaf." Then his brothers said to him, "Are you actually going to reign over us? Or are you really going to rule over us?" So* they hated him even more *for his dreams and for his words. Now he had still another dream, and related it to his brothers, and said, "Lo, I have had still another dream; and behold, the sun and the moon and eleven stars were bowing down to me." He related it to his father and to his brothers; and his father rebuked him and said to him, "What is this dream that you have had? Shall I and your mother and your brothers actually come to bow ourselves down before you to the ground?" His brothers were jealous of him, but his father kept the saying in mind. (Gen. 37:5–11)*

Talk about rubbing salt in an already festering wound! Dreams always need an interpretation as we will see later in this story and in other stories of dreams throughout the Old Testament. But that didn't happen here in the midst of a haughty conversation.

When he finished bragging on his dreams, the brothers *hated* him. That's a very strong word used to describe their feelings for a sibling. Weren't brothers supposed to love each other? After all, wasn't he special? He certainly thought he was special. And why would God give him these dreams if he weren't special? Can you feel it? Can you feel their incensed anger? Wouldn't you have felt the same way? They had had about enough of this kid! Wasn't "dislike" a strong enough word? Why "hate"? This was probably not the first time they had talked among themselves about this spoiled kid. It was more like the hundredth time even before it's stated in the story! (Gen. 37: 5, 8, 11)

My question here is this: why didn't they hate their father because of the way Joseph was treated? Psychologically they did, but this was a patriarchal society and the father was "king." You didn't go against your father. So this hatred was squarely placed on the sibling. A child doesn't quite know what to do with hatred toward a father. They do know what to do with that hatred when it is toward a sibling. They just want to get rid of the thing that is causing so much pain and animosity. Siblings hate those closest in age to them if they are treated differently.

Sibling Rivalry: As Old as Time

Sibling rivalry is nothing new. Cain killed Abel because of jealousy. In this instance it was God who was involved, but I wonder, were they treated differently by their parents? After all, Cain was the very first human son. Was he special and because of that, should his offering not be acceptable as well as Abel's? Maybe he was always treated special by his parents. Maybe he got his way all too often. If he was treated differently, he probably felt whatever he did should be acceptable, not only to his parents but to God. God had cursed the ground because of Adam's sin so a sacrifice from the ground would never have been accepted, no matter who brought it. Did Cain feel he was special and that God should accept that he offered his best, even though it was not what God clearly instructed? Shouldn't his best account for something?

Ishmael and Isaac were never close brothers, and it caused a rift that still occurs today between Arab and Jew. Jacob and Esau, twin brothers, shared the same animosity toward each other. Sibling rivalry was the only thing they knew. David was a younger brother in his family. In that instance he was ignored as one too young to count for anything, especially a position of king!

In most families there are comments of one child receiving more favors by the parent. Kids notice. They did then, they do now. Human nature has not changed, no matter the era or the circumstances. If some children get a college degree, while others do not, there could be jealousy. If one child has a good marriage, and another does not, there might be envy. If a sibling marries a spouse not liked or respected by another sibling, there is hurt. If grandchildren are treated differently, the parents notice. We must always be aware of our own family dynamics and how dysfunctional we all are. We have a tendency to think that we are right and we see things right, when often that is not the case. Aren't we all flawed human beings? It's amazing that we survive at all living together with such animosity in our hearts. What is that verse, "Our hearts are deceitful above all things" (Jer. 17:9)? My heart? No. Your heart! Couldn't be *my* heart.

I mentioned earlier that wounded people wound people. When we are wounded time after time, it is wound upon wound, too many layers to deal with. So we want to crawl in a hole and not deal with it. We all get wounded. It's what we do with the wounds that make a difference in our futures. Sometimes counseling will help peel back the layers of hurt so that we can put all the wounds on the table and see them for what they are. Our Savior was wounded beyond belief, but He had the perspective that those wounds are for our healing. He heals. We don't. He has perspective. He can give us perspective. You will see how I believe Joseph dealt with his wounds later in the book.

If you've been hurt beyond what you think you can bear, ask God for perspective. He will give it to you without withholding grace. Some of us reading this book are sensitive in nature. We get hurt easily. Others of us are more insensitive and therefore take hurt more in stride. It doesn't mean insensitive people don't get hurt. Insensitive people are accused all the time of not caring. They do care. But sensitive people tend to dwell more deeply and maybe longer when hurt.

The other issue that Scripture is clear on is the sins of the father being passed to the next generations. What we grow up with, we learn. We learn behavior. We learn values. We learn morals. We then pass those on to our children and our grandchildren. Rebellion in the fathers is clear. Listen to these words about passing on to future generations.

> *For He established a testimony in Jacob*
> *And appointed a law in Israel,*
> *Which He commanded our fathers*
> *That they should teach them to their children,*
> *That the generation to come might know, even the*
> *children yet to be born,*

That they may arise and tell them to their children,
That they should put their confidence in God
And not forget the works of God,
But keep His commandments,
And not be like their fathers,
A stubborn and rebellious generation,
A generation that did not prepare its heart
And whose spirit was not faithful to God.
(Ps. 78:5–8)

I believe the psalmist is here talking about the sins of Jacob being passed to his sons and grandsons. Had Joseph stayed in the family compound, he may have become like his brothers. He certainly had already picked up issues from his father. Did God simply pick him up and carry him away to another culture, much different than his own, to learn a language he didn't know, to get acquainted with a different people? What was God's purpose in removing Joseph? His story will unfold now as we walk through the next years of his life.

We know that it was God who gave Joseph the dreams while he was an arrogant seventeen-year-old kid. He knew the brothers would react the way they did. Did God use their jealousy and hatred to remove Joseph from the family? I believe He did. God had a plan for Joseph. But He also had a plan for the whole clan of Israel.

Remember, God's plan cannot be thwarted by Satan or mankind, no matter the circumstances or the obstacles put in the way. His plan will be accomplished. There was work to be done in Joseph. But there was also work to be done with the brothers and the father. God will tell us what He is doing in the life of Joseph. But it would be foolish indeed to think that He was not also working in the "sons of disobedience."

We must ask the question: what were the strengths and weaknesses of Joseph? How was God going to use and mature him to be a man of God? Here is a comment made by my friend, Beth English (February 2015):

> Every strength is given for the good of the whole, and not for personal power. There is fragility in the strengths we are given. Our giftedness can be easily misused, because of our bent toward sin. Our strengths can become unbalanced. It is therefore important to walk closely with God and not try to manage our strengths on our own. Our strengths can be exaggerated or overused because we do not demonstrate a restraining use of power as God does. For instance, one in authority could use his power to lead and serve others, but that same power can be exaggerated to "lord it over" others. A negative behavior is the downside of a strength. A strong-willed child can be oppositional, but he/she is also demonstrating great perseverance.

Strengths and weaknesses are used by God to benefit our lives. Joseph had great strengths (we will find out what those were in future chapters). He also had weaknesses. How did God use others in his areas of weakness?

Questions for Chapter 3

1) What were you like as a teen?

2) Was there sibling rivalry in your home?

3) If you have had a teenager in your home, describe your relationship. Do you identify with Joseph?

4) Have you been wounded by a family member? Has it been "patched up" or is it still festering?

5) If you know how one or both of your parents experienced wounding, can you elaborate here?

6) What are your strengths and weaknesses? How have those been used by God in your life?

CHAPTER 4

HOW DOES GOD SPEAK?

We must break our train of thought on the life of Joseph for clarification of how God speaks throughout human history. We know God spoke directly to Joseph in dreams when he was a teen, but He will also use other's dreams to demonstrate His will. God is the same yesterday, today, and forever. He does not change. His methods of speaking to us, His children, take different forms in progressive revelation throughout time.

God used dreams and their interpretations numerous times in the Old Testament to various people (Abraham, Jacob, Joseph, Isaiah, Daniel, etc.) How do we look at the dreams and their interpretations in scripture? All of us dream when in our REM sleep patterns. That is common. What divides our nightly dreams from "God-speaking" dreams? Dreams in Scripture were prophetical in nature. They foretold what would either soon take place or some future event.

Throughout history God has used many different ways to communicate to His people. What did they have before the scriptures were canonized? They had writings (stories) and genealogy from previous generations. How did Moses write Genesis when he wasn't even alive? The story of Adam was already written. Noah would have had documents of history that he took on the ark with him. Noah would have recorded his own story of the flood. The story of Abraham, Isaac, and Jacob would have also been in written form. Journaling is not a modern concept. We have biblical books filled with the lives of real people.

Look at these verses out of Genesis for confirmation that records were kept and passed down from one generation to the next. I believe these were written, not oral records. Moses compiled this information when writing the book of Genesis.

Written Records

This is the account *of the heavens and the earth when they were created, in the day that the Lord God made earth and heaven. (God gave Adam the information) (Gen. 2:4)*

This is the book *of the generations* of Adam. *(Gen. 5:1)*

These are the records of *the generations of* Noah. *(Gen. 6:9)*

These are the records of *the generations of* Shem. *(Gen. 11:10)*

Now these are the records *of the generations of* Terah. *(Gen. 11:27)*

These are the records *of the generations of* Ishmael. *(Gen. 25:12)*

These are the records of the generations of Isaac.
(Gen. 25:19)

These are the records of the generations of Esau.
(Gen. 36:1)

These are the records of the generations of Jacob.
(Gen. 37:2)

These record the names of tribes coming out of
Egypt. (Exod. 1:1–14)

God gave Moses direct revelation concerning creation and the early history of mankind. Moses then simply compiled historical records as the Spirit of God directed him. In the early chapters of Exodus, he wrote about the years of slavery in Egypt, then his own birth story, his adoption by Pharaoh's daughter, and his later identification with his own people—the Israelites. Exodus records what happened in his lifetime before the people enter into the Promised Land.

The Israelite tribes did not have the written Scriptures as we have today. The Scriptures were progressively given to writers. Moses compiled Genesis but wrote Exodus through Deuteronomy. Other authors began to record their histories and later those recordings became some of the books of the Old Testament. By Jesus's day, the Old Testament was "canonized" and put in scroll/book form. Jesus read from "the Scriptures."

So how did God speak to people thousands of years before the Bible was canonized? How did He tell them what to do? He did it through dreams and visions, as well as historical documents. He spoke audibly to them as He did with Abraham, Jacob, Joseph, Moses, and others.

God has always spoken to us in our consciences. How many times in your own life have you been struggling with a decision? You don't have clear direction, either from others or from Scripture. And yet, in your conscience you weigh the issues and make a decision based on logic. If it is wrong, God will intervene. If not, you go ahead with the decisions you made. It happens all the time. God gave us a mind. He uses our mind to direct us when no clear direction is in front of us.

For thousands of years, before Moses was given the laws, they would have had genealogical records and written records of lives. But they also had a God who spoke audibly, or through angels or dreams. The prophets hadn't come along yet to warn of the future. The Messiah had not come to show us definitively what it means to be saved and how that was to happen. But that does not mean God was silent. Faith was clearly spoken of and defined in the earliest parts of Genesis. All who put their trust in Yahweh for salvation were called people of faith. It says of Abraham, *"Abraham believed God, and it was credited to him as righteousness"* (Rom. 4:3).

How Does God Speak: Then and Now

Genealogies were recorded and kept by family clans. There must have been some "rules or laws" that were written on the heart of mankind. But beyond that, how did Joseph know what to do and not to do? Our hearts convince or convict us. The Holy Spirit has always been in operation, both Old and New Testament times, but the directions from the Holy Spirit would have come in visions and dreams. The Bible is clear when it says that Jesus is the same yesterday, today, and forever. Yesterday means just that—all the days, months, years and eras before the coming of Jesus the Messiah. If He was the same in Joseph's time as He is in ours, then it stands to reason that God revealed Himself to Joseph, much as He does to us today, in our hearts. Today we confirm it with Scripture, because our hearts can be deceptive. In Joseph's time, he must have relied on his heart, his conscience, visions, dreams, and God's voice. We still have all those things available to us today, but we don't rely on visions and dreams as much because we have the written Word of God.

Today in Muslim cultures, where the Bible is banned, it is not uncommon for God to come to people in visions and dreams to tell them who He is. One of the foremost organizations that has a multitude of testimonies to this effect is the Jesus Film Project. Stories abound where dreams and visions are *the* main tool God uses to bring truth to Muslim people groups.

God Is Unchanging, Therefore His Methods of Speaking Are Unchanging

I am the Lord; I do not change. (Mal. 3:6)

Holy, holy, holy is the Lord God, the Almighty, who was and who is and who is to come. *(Rev. 4:8)*

Because we have the Word of God, His voice comes primarily through the Scriptures and we don't need to rely on Him speaking to us in visions and dreams. However, He still can and does speak in numerous ways to us, including dreams. Many things change from year to year and era to era. But one thing never changes: Almighty God. We can be assured that He was the same God who spoke to Joseph as speaks to us today. God's characteristics never change. He is always love and peace. He is always just. He will always have our best interest at heart, no matter the situation. Because He doesn't change, I can count on Him to do what is right, regardless of how I feel or think.

The way of salvation has not changed. How people of the Old Testament understood salvation was "veiled," but faith in God was clear.

> *So then those who are* of faith *are blessed with* Abraham, *the believer. (Gal. 3:9)*

> *For the promise to* Abraham *or to his descendants that he would be heir* of *the world was not through the Law, but through the righteousness* of faith. *(Rom. 4:130)*

> *Jesus said to him, "I am the way, and the truth, and the life;* no one *comes to the Father but through Me. (John 14:6)*

> *Of Him* all the prophets bear witness *that through His name everyone who believes in Him receives forgiveness of sins. (Acts 10:43)*

> *Therefore having overlooked the times of ignorance, God is now declaring to men that all people everywhere should repent. (Acts 17:30)*

In Old Testament times they knew about the Messiah who was to come one day and take away the sins of the world. They put their faith in God and His promises.

I have listed below the different ways God speaks, both in times past and also today. His nature never changes. This is a good Bible study to go through if you are in doubt about how God speaks and uses other believers to help you make decisions. Some verses are written out. Others you may want to look up.

- Through Nature

  - o *For since the creation of the world His invisible attributes, His eternal power and divine nature, have been clearly seen, being* understood through what has been made, *so that they are without excuse. (Rom. 1:20)*
  - o Psalm 19:1–2

- Through Consciences

  - o *I am telling the truth in Christ, I am not lying, my* conscience testifies *with me in the Holy Spirit. (Rom. 9:1)*

- Dreams and Visions:

  - o *God spoke to Israel in visions of the night and said, "Jacob, Jacob." And he said, "Here I am." (Gen. 46:2)*
    In a dream, a vision of the night,
    When sound sleep falls on men,
    While they slumber in their beds.
    (Job 33:15)
  - o *In the year of King Uzziah's death I saw the Lord sitting on a throne, lofty and exalted, with the train of His robe filling the temple. Seraphim stood above Him, each having six wings: with two he covered his face, and with two he covered his feet, and with two he flew. And one called out to another and said,*
    "Holy, Holy, Holy, is the Lord of hosts,
    The whole earth is full of His glory."
    (Isa. 6:1–3)
  - o Daniel 2:19–23, 30, 47, 7:15, 8:1, 15
  - o Joel 2:28

- o   Lamentations 2:14
- o   Genesis 37:5–10
- o   1 Kings 3:5–15
- o   Matthew 1:20, 2:13, 19
- o   Acts 10:9–16; 16:9

- Audible voice

  - o   *When the Lord saw that he turned aside to look,* God called to him *from the midst of the bush and said, "Moses, Moses!" And he said, "Here I am." (Exod. 3:4)*
  - o   1 Samuel 3:4–6
  - o   Acts 9:34

- Through Music

  - o   Psalms is full of praise music
  - o   Listening to our radio or TV in praise
  - o   *You need not fight in this battle; station yourselves, stand and see the salvation of the Lord on your behalf... When he had consulted with the people, he appointed those who sang to the Lord and those who praised Him in holy attire, as they went out before the army and said, "Give thanks to the Lord, for His lovingkindness is everlasting." When* they began singing and praising, *the Lord set ambushes against the sons of Ammon, Moab and Mount Seir, who had come against Judah (2 Chrons 20:17-22)*

- Through the Written Word

  - o   Matthew 24:35

o   Psalm 119:105

o   *From childhood you have known the sacred writings which are able to give you the wisdom that leads to salvation through faith which is in Christ Jesus. All* Scripture is inspired by God *and profitable for teaching, for reproof, for correction, for training in righteousness. (2 Tim. 3:15)*

o   *For whatever was written in earlier times was written for our instruction, so that through perseverance and the encouragement of the Scriptures we might have hope. (Rom. 15:4)*

o   Acts 17:1

o   Matthew 4:1–10

o   *The Word of God* stands forever. *(Isa. 40:8)*

- Through His Son, Jesus Christ

o   *In the beginning was the Word, and the Word was with God, and the Word was God. He was in the beginning with God. All things came into being through Him, and apart from Him nothing came into being that has come into being. In Him was life, and the life was the Light of men. (John 1:1–4)*

o   *God, after He spoke long ago to the fathers in the prophets in many portions and in many ways, in these last days has* spoken to us in His Son, *whom He appointed heir of all things, through whom also He made the world. (Heb. 1:1–2)*

o   John 10:27

- Through the Holy Spirit (Spirit of God, Spirit of Christ)

  o *And there was a man in Jerusalem whose name was Simeon; and this man was righteous and devout, looking for the consolation of Israel; and the Holy Spirit was upon him. And it had been* revealed to him by the Holy Spirit *that he would not see death before he had seen the Lord's Christ. (Luke 2:25–26)*
  o John 14:17; 26, 16:13
  o 1 Corinthians 2:9–12, 3:16
  o 1 Peter 1:6–14

- Through other believers

  o *But the wisdom from above is first pure, then peaceable, gentle, reasonable, full of mercy and good fruits, unwavering, without hypocrisy. (James 3:17)*
  o Romans 12:6–8
  o Job 33:14

- Through circumstances

  o Before I was afflicted *I went astray, but now I keep Your word. You are good and do good: Teach me Your statues. (Ps. 119:67)*

- Through prayer

  o *In the same way the Spirit also helps our weakness; for* we do not know how to pray *as we should, but the Spirit Himself intercedes for us with groanings too deep for words; and He who searches the hearts knows what the mind of the Spirit is, because He intercedes for the saints according to the will of God. (Rom. 8:26–27)*

- Other ways: preaching, teaching, friendship

  o *So faith comes from hearing, and hearing by the word of Christ. (Rom 10:17)*

  o *And every day, in the temple and from house to house, they kept right on teaching and preaching Jesus as the Christ. (Acts 5:42)*

  o *Faithful are the wounds of a friend,*
    But deceitful are the kisses of an enemy.
    (Prov. 27:6)

- Through painful trials

  o *Consider it all joy, my brethren, when you encounter various trials, knowing that the testing of your faith produces endurance. And let endurance have its perfect result, so that you may be perfect and complete, lacking in nothing. (James 1:2–4)*

  o *In this you greatly rejoice, even though now for a little while, if necessary, you have been distressed by various trials (1 Pet.)*

Through miracles

  o *As He passed by, He saw a man blind from birth. And His disciples asked Him, "Rabbi, who sinned, this man or his parents, that he would be born blind?" Jesus answered, "It was neither that this man sinned, nor his parents; but it was* so that the works of God might be displayed *in him. (John 9:2–3)*

Waiting on God

o *For the vision is yet for the appointed time;*
   It hastens toward the goal and it will not fail.
   Though it tarries, wait for it;
   For it will certainly come, it will not delay.
   (Hab. 2:3)

God uses many methods to speak to us. When we don't feel anything is happening, wait, be patient. God will never contradict His Word, and the messages He gives will always bring glory to Himself. And it will be in His timing, not necessarily in ours. Joseph had dreams at age seventeen. They were not fulfilled until age thirty-nine. Wow! That's a long time to wait. God often teaches and trains us while we wait. Remember, He is not in a hurry as we often are.

Meditating on Scripture is a beneficial way to "listen" to the Lord. Carefully check guidance we receive through other people with the Word of God. We are capable of being deceived. Waiting is beneficial when no clear direction is in front of us.

The Bible also warns about adding anything to the already written, God-breathed Word of God, or accepting any other messenger who claims to be superior to Jesus.

I testify to everyone who hears the words of the prophecy of this book: if anyone adds to them, God will add to him the plagues which are written in this book; and if anyone takes away from the words of the book of this prophecy, God will take away his part from the tree of life and from the holy city, which are written in this book. (Rev. 22:18–19)

For if one comes and preaches another Jesus whom we have not preached, or you receive a different spirit which you have not received, or a different gospel which you have not accepted, you bear this beautifully. (2 Cor. 11:4)

God Spoke to Joseph in Dreams

Because Joseph did not have the written Word of God, God would have used other means to speak to him and to people around him. This was quite common in the Old Testament writings. Many of the above ideas were also used by God to speak to His people.

What we have before us in the young life of Joseph is God warning his people of a severe economic time ahead and how they would survive through it. Neither Joseph nor his brothers understood the dreams nor gave any thought to interpretations.

Genesis 37:5–9 states the two dreams Joseph told to his brothers. Dream One:

"Please listen to this dream which I have had; for behold, we were binding sheaves in the field, and lo, my sheaf rose up and also stood erect; and behold, your sheaves gathered around and bowed down to my sheaf."

Then his brothers said to him, "Are you actually going to reign over us? Or are you really going to rule over us?" So they hated him even more for his dreams and for his words.

Dream Two:

Now he had still another dream, and related it to his brothers, and said, "Lo, I have had still another dream; and behold, the sun and the moon and eleven stars were bowing down to me."

We see an undiscerning seventeen-year-old kid bragging to his brothers about his position of authority in the future. He did not, nor did his brothers, try to figure out what the dreams meant. If he had asked God for an interpretation, God would have revealed that a severe famine was coming, the likes of which they had never seen (the sheaves speak of economic collapse). But that's not what he emphasized and that's not what the brothers heard. The brothers heard that their younger kid brother was going to be elevated above them and their parents (the sun, moon, and eleven stars). The issue of his authority must have galled them to the core. He was, after all, the younger brother. In their culture the eldest son was always the object of elevation through the birth order. Reuben was the eldest, Joseph the eleventh son.

Joseph did not have the discernment to analyze the dreams and warn the brothers of impending doom. All that came out of it was his own importance. No wonder they hated him. They had had enough of this prideful, spoiled brat of a brother! Most siblings would have reacted the same. Obviously Joseph had told his father before going out to the brothers in the fields.

It appears that he had other dreams before this. Listen to what it says:

His brothers were jealous of him, but his father kept the saying in mind. (vs. 37:11)

They said to one another, "Here comes this dreamer!
(vs. 19)

This was not the first time the brothers heard dreams from Joseph. Evidentially there were other dreams not recorded here. It says his father kept the sayings in mind, *Those other dreams?* Also, it says the brothers were jealous. Of what? Of his dreams? Of his being favored? Of his fantasies? Maybe all of the above.

Questions for Chapter 4

1)   List characteristics of God that never change. Why is this important?

2)   Look at the above verses on ways God speaks. How many of those have you experienced?

3)   Why don't we put much emphasis on dreams and visions today? Have you ever had a dream or vision that has come true?

CHAPTER 5

FAMILY WOUNDS

Now then, come and let us kill him *and throw him into one of the pits; and we will say, 'A wild beast devoured him.' Then let us see what will become of his dreams!" But Reuben heard this and rescued him out of their hands and said, "Let us not take his life." Reuben further said to them, "Shed no blood. Throw him into this pit that is in the wilderness, but do not lay hands on him"— (that he might rescue him out of their hands, to restore him to his father). So it came about, when Joseph reached his brothers, that they stripped Joseph of his tunic, the varicolored tunic that was on him; and they took him and threw him into the pit. Now the pit was empty, without any water in it. Then they sat down to eat a meal. And as they raised their eyes and looked, behold, a caravan of Ishmaelites was coming from Gilead, with their camels bearing aromatic gum and balm and myrrh, on their way to bring them down to Egypt. Judah said to his brothers, "What profit is it for us to kill our brother and cover up his blood? Come and let us sell him to the Ishmaelites and not lay our hands on him, for he is our brother, our own flesh." And his brothers listened to him. Then some Midianite traders passed by, so they pulled him up and lifted Joseph out of the pit, and sold him to the Ishmaelites for twenty shekels of silver. Thus they brought Joseph into Egypt. (Gen. 37:20–28)*

Price of a Slave

If it be from five years even to twenty years old then your valuation for the male shall be twenty shekels and for the female ten shekels. (Lev. 27:5)

"Let's kill him!" We are not told which brother said that. Reuben, the eldest, heard this and wanted to come later to rescue him. That will play a significant role later on in the story. When Judah saw a caravan coming, he said, "Let's sell him." Only Reuben and Judah are mentioned by name at this stage in Joseph's life. Reuben wanted nothing to do with the plot. He was the eldest, and the responsibility for all the brothers fell to him. Judah saw a way to rid their family of Joseph by making a profit on him.

I am sure Joseph pleaded with his brothers. We are not told, but don't you think this teen begged for his life and promised to be better? That's what teens do. The brothers simply went far enough away so they couldn't hear his cries for help and glibly ate their lunch. (Okay, maybe Joseph thought that he would wait till the brothers were gone, and then he would dig out of this pit and go back home with another story of how bad his brothers were. He would wait.)

But God had other plans. Joseph was never meant to go back home. God was literally removing Joseph from this dysfunctional family into which he was born.

> *Now Reuben returned to the pit, and behold, Joseph was not in the pit; so he tore his garments. He returned to his brothers and said, "The boy is not there; as for me, where am I to go?" So they took Joseph's tunic, and slaughtered a male goat and dipped the tunic in the blood; and they sent the varicolored tunic and brought it to their father and said, "We found this; please examine it to see whether it is your son's tunic or not." Then he examined it and said, "It is my son's tunic. A wild beast has devoured him; Joseph has surely been torn to pieces!" So Jacob tore his clothes, and put sackcloth on his loins and mourned for his son many days. Then all his sons and all his daughters arose to comfort him, but he refused to be comforted. And he said, "Surely I will go down to Sheol in mourning for my son." So his father wept for him.* (Gen. 37:29–35)

The Depth of Deception

After Joseph was sold, the brothers had to cover for their misdeed. Instead of telling the truth (chip off the old block), they now had to make up a story, tell their father, and try to go on with life as if nothing had happened. How difficult it must have been when ten brothers are sworn to secrecy, and they actually pulled this off for the next twenty years. How often must they have thought about telling the truth, but couldn't or wouldn't. They watched their aging father despairing in his grief. They had to go through the long period of mourning and "fake" being sad.

Not only that, some of the ten brothers either had wives and children by this time so they also had to either keep the secret from their wives or tell them and swear them to secrecy. What a burdensome thing to carry a secret as monumental as that with so many people involved in the plot. With two people it's difficult enough to keep a secret, but with ten or twenty or more (family members), that would be exhausting!

We know in our own generation how difficult it is to cover up for something that happened. We now have forensics. We have DNA. We have TV and reporters who uncover truth or hide truth in skewed reporting. It amazes me how often on TV we see someone who has told a lie and covers it up and continues to lie to cover up the cover up. We are amazing human beings, aren't we? At all costs, don't get caught! But if you do, lie some more. I am sure the brothers looked at each other every family gathering, hoping no one would "crack" and tell the truth to their dad. They didn't. Amazing!

What about Jacob's Heart?

Do we ever stop to think about Jacob losing a child? You can read between the lines to know that I am not fond of Jacob as a man, a man who manipulated and connived his whole life to get what he wanted.

But one thing we must recognize is his loss at this point. Any parent who has ever lost a child, no matter the age, suffers tremendously. Jacob was still suffering twenty years later from the grief of loss when he will once again see his beloved son. Jacob grieved the loss of Rachel, so dear to him. Now he will suffer the loss of his beloved son Joseph, whom he fears died a horrible death, being torn and eaten by a wild animal. We cannot see into his soul because the Bible is silent here except to say his mourning and grieving were very real. The loss of a child has to be one of the most devastating any person has to endure. The loss clouds the rest of life. It permeates everything we do.

This is an area that Jacob can't manipulate and fix. He is devastated beyond his capacity to understand. He manipulated and fixed his birthright over Esau. He manipulated and fixed his marriage to Rachel. He later manipulated and fixed his meeting with Esau. He can't fix this one. Did this loss of Joseph change his heart? We are not told. We only know that his loss carried excruciating pain, as it does for all parents who lose a child. So we mourn with Jacob. We who know the rest of the story know the end. But Jacob did not. His loss was deep, agonizing, and prolonged.

Did he ask God why? I am sure he did. Did he play the "what if" game? I am sure he did. And the brothers knew, but they have conspired to not tell. How sad to watch your heartbroken father, whom you could alleviate with the truth, but you are sworn to secrecy? How difficult it must have been for this already dysfunctional family?

But God knew that if Jacob had been told the truth, he would have moved heaven and earth to find Joseph. He would have spent his fortune to bring him home. God, however, was in control. God needed to separate Joseph from his family to teach him to stand on his own in following God. God didn't allow any of the brothers to spill the beans and tell Jacob. Time wore on. It was never far from Jacob's mind or from the brother's minds. Never forgotten, just covered up and not talked about.

Wounds Come

Remember this phrase through the rest of the book: woundedness comes, not from someone or something you don't love, it comes from someone or something you *do* or did love. Joseph loved his brothers, even though he was arrogant and young and foolish.

I personally cannot imagine a sibling wanting to murder another one. I understand wanting to get rid of them for a day or two, but not murder. This story of these brothers and their hatred is a deep and dramatic one. Joseph must have sensed what his brothers thought of him. But murder? I am sure he was bewildered with the extent of their negativity toward him.

Where have your family wounds come from? Were you one of millions of young women who were abused at the hands of a trusted male relative? Your scars run deep. Abuse has affected your life forever. How have you dealt with such incredible hurt?

Maybe your wound is not abuse but a sibling who has been or said some cruel things that have cut you to the quick. Maybe it's a grown sibling or parent who keeps wounding you with cutting remarks. You love that person, but for the most part, you really don't like them and it's difficult to be around them.

Family wounds have a way of "sticking" around because you have to see that person from time to time. Has your parent been the "needy" one who always makes you feel guilty for your lack of involvement? You try, but it never gets any better.

Then there are the wounds that come in every single marriage on planet earth. Husbands and wives have such an intimate connection that when things go badly in marriage, it affects their entire lives. Some marriages go through much hurt and confusion, and situations are never resolved to either one's satisfaction. Separation, divorce, and split custody of children are a by-product of wounds that are never healed. Most marriages are in some state of wounding or repairing all the time. This book isn't about marriage but there will be some helpful references in the back of the book. Don and I highly recommend marriage counseling if you find you are in need of a third party's ear. Make sure the counselors understand Scripture on marriage.

We all have family problems because we are fallen people. Joseph's brothers took a drastic measure to get rid of the thorn in their flesh. But you will notice later in the story how bad they felt about their early actions. It haunted each of them for years. They never got over the wound they inflicted upon their brother. Know that those who wound and those they wound always know what happened. It's always in the back of their minds. At times they feel they have forgotten, and then a memory surfaces to remind them of the wound.

Joseph and his brothers were normal. They were just like us. So we must see this story to the end. All of them had to get through their own wounds. That they had a dark secret between them only caused them to hide their wounds even more. So many families cover up sins in the family. Many shove problems under the rug, hoping they won't surface. When they do arise, they shove further. Many people don't know how to get in touch with their emotions and ignore hurts and wounds either done to them or that they inflict on others. "If you don't talk about it, it isn't there." It doesn't work. Eventually, things will surface when you least expect them to and dealing with them is difficult when lack of communication has been a way of life in your family.

A Parable of Three Sons (A True Story)

Many years ago a father had three sons. Times were bleak, and the world was in the throes of the Great Depression. The first and second son left elementary school in the fourth grade to find a job to help with family finances. They each found work, and they worked hard and long for the family. The third son was ten years younger so never had to work. Not only that, but whatever the third son wanted he got, even though times were tough. The first two sons didn't like that he was treated differently, but they were older and so tried to understand.

Time wore on, and all three sons grew up and got married. Even though the father was poor, he had accumulated three acres of land. All three sons' families were poor. But the middle son was trying to stand on his own two feet and bought a shack in the mountains and proceeded to fix it up for his family.

The father decided to give his three acres away to his sons. He gave the oldest son one acre so he could build a house. He gave the youngest son two acres right next door for him to build a house. To the middle son he gave nothing.

Which son grew up to hate his father? Not just because of the acres of land but because the youngest was the favored among them and things were constantly given to him that were not given to the other two sons.

This is a true story. My father was that middle son who grew to hate his father. Why? Prejudice, favoritism, and injustice created hatred. Dad was wounded over and over again by his father. It never went away. He had a cordial relationship with his father but was never close to him. He never confided in him or told him in any way that he loved him. I don't recall my father ever communicating with his dad on any issue except surface issues. There was no heartfelt communication between them. The hurt ran deep.

Some people have struggled all their lives with a wound in childhood. Or that wound came later in life when a parent or sibling said or did something hurtful. When there is a lack of communication, no matter the struggle, wounds have a way of sticking around for a long time. All of us have been wounded by family, some more deeply than others. This is the human condition we live in. It was true in biblical times; it is true today.

Questions for Chapter 5

1) Have you and your siblings talked about wounds that have been inflicted by each other? Has there been resolve?

2) You may have experienced wounds from your parent. Has there been resolve there?

3) Have you experienced marital wounds? Has there been resolve and changing of your marriage?

4) Have you or someone you know lost a child? What is the best way to come along side that person?

5) Talk about lies, either from you or another, why is it difficult to keep a secret?

6) What effect does lying have on communication? Has that occurred in your relationships?

CHAPTER 6

WORKPLACE WOUNDS

Meanwhile, the Midianites sold him in Egypt to Potiphar, Pharaoh's officer, the captain of the bodyguard. (Gen. 37:36)

God had already given Joseph the dreams. He knew the future as He knows the past. With God it's as though the future has already taken place. God knew there was a severe famine coming. He needed to protect the Messianic lineage. He needed a Hebrew in authority in Egypt in order for that protection to take place. God had to get one of the brothers to Egypt. How was He going to do that, and which one would it be? God looks at the heart. God knew that in Joseph He could mold a young man for His purposes. Inside of Joseph there must have been a pliable heart that was tender toward the things of God.

God sees not as man sees, for man looks at the outward appearance, but the Lord looks at the heart. (1 Sam. 16:7b)

Joseph's life had to be spared because he was going to be used to alter the course of the entire family. But first, God had work to do in Joseph's life.

The Ishmaelites paid cash for this strapping young man because they knew they could turn a profit. Because we know the ending of the story, we tend to fall asleep here and yawn. But don't. You will miss the process God took Joseph through to make him what he would ultimately become. He didn't know that. God knew what it would take to change this young man's life from one of pride and boasting to one of humility.

The Purpose of God

I believe God had to remove Joseph from this incredibly dysfunctional family. Here was a father who manipulated and connived his whole life, being influenced by his family of origin, and then modeled those same characteristics to his sons. Here was a group of women who vied for the attention of Jacob and did whatever was necessary to cheat and usurp the others. Here was a group of brothers, although they seemed to have camaraderie, probably would stab the other in the back given the chance. We won't go into their lives here except to say they were a ruthless bunch of brothers. Simeon and Levi killed a whole village of men (Gen. 34) because one of those men raped their sister Dinah. Reuben slept with his father's concubine (Gen. 35:22) and brought the wrath of the father upon him. Judah had his own problems with disobedient sons whom God destroyed (Gen. 38). These older brothers weren't living "godly" lives by any stretch of the imagination.

So removing Joseph while he was still in the pliable teen years was very important. God had to get him to stand on his own and learn to walk with Him. He would use a series of tests to help him do that.

Making Faith Our Own

Have you ever wondered in your own life why it's important to make your faith your own and not the faith of your parents? Why is it important to pass some really tough tests while you are young? Has that happened to you? I left home at eighteen and went off to college. There were some pretty tough tests in learning to walk with God. My own father was not a believer, and when I went to college, he would make a statement like "You think you're so smart just because you are in college." Now I don't remember thinking that, but I must have come across to my father, who had a ninth-grade education, as appearing arrogant. I don't know what I said or did for him to think that. But something in my behavior demonstrated my immaturity. I understand that now, but didn't back then.

Temptations came strongly in college. I was away from home. I had freedom to go, do, and be. There were times I came way to close to crossing the line. I am not proud of those times, but they were there for my testing. Do you ever wonder why age seventeen to eighteen is crucial both for you and for your children? This must be an age where God can either get our attention or we will choose to go our own way, no matter the consequences. Think about when you left home. Think about what happened in your own life during those years between the time you left home and either graduated from college, started a career, or married and started a family.

For many of us, we forged our own way. Some experimented with drugs, alcohol, and sex. What were the conclusions of those years? We may have also declared our major in college, which motivated us for the next segment of our lives. If we didn't go to college, we either got a job, married, and began a family, or all of the above. These ten years in our lives were pivotal to everything that has happened to us since: who we dated, who we married, what our vocation became. These three issues determined the course of the rest of our lives. The trials we went through, the people we dated and broke up with, the colleges we attended and the majors we chose—all played a part in what we became. I think it is no accident that the late teens are important years for us physically, emotionally, but, especially, spiritually.

I want to interject here how God "calls" us or works in our lives. For me, I cannot remember a time in my life where God was not real. As a young child I knew God existed. I also knew He had His hand on my life. I didn't understand spiritual things, but I always felt that nudge toward a life following Him. You may have experienced the same thing. At one point you began to understand salvation. At other times you understood the Holy Spirit. Scripture was always important. I cannot remember a time I didn't love going to God's Word and getting direction from Him.

In the sixties, while working on the college campus, we encountered a slogan that said, "God is dead." It was in a very turbulent time in our country when love was touted to be "free" and "God is dead" so go ahead and experiment. What we found on the college campus was a hundred eighty degrees from that statement. Some kids wanted the freedom to follow the crowd. But many were saddened by the blatant shunning of God. Students responded by the droves to the idea that God was indeed "alive." They responded to the idea of a God of love and peace and a God, who as a Father, disciplines His children. They learned to follow Him. Those were great years when students were defining who they were, what they would become, and Who they would follow. A mighty student movement was created because they saw through the fog of rhetoric that made no sense. It was called the Jesus Movement. Many of the students had lives dramatically changed and are now in ministry, businesses, and homes influencing others to follow Christ.

The opposite also happened in the sixties. This was a time of political unrest and secular violence. The "free" love appeal infected the college students of that day. Morals went by the wayside. They didn't like the government. They didn't like the establishment. They didn't like their parents' morals. So they continued their rebellion. Many of those students who displayed unrest in the sixties now run our country. They are a generation of entitlement thinkers who rail against the rich (although a good many are wealthy by any world standard) and are now touting that the government can provide equality and social programs. They say they are for the poor, but if they had to live by the standards of the poor, they would rail against that too.

Whenever Satan has an idea to thwart the plan and purposes of God, God comes in, matches him head to head and always comes out on top. We saw that firsthand in the turbulent sixties. We are still seeing that today. When people rightly see the love of God, rightly see that His plan is best for them, and rightly see how to follow Him, they do. I think of the parable of the sower that Jesus told his disciples.

> *Then He left the crowds and went into the house. And His disciples came to Him and said, "Explain to us the parable of the tares of the field." And He said, "The one who sows the good seed is the Son of Man, and the field is the world; and as for the good seed, these are the sons of the kingdom; and the tares are the sons of the evil one; and the enemy who sowed them is the devil, and the harvest is the end of the age; and the reapers are angels. So just as the tares are gathered up and burned with fire, so shall it be at the end of the age. The Son of Man will send forth His angels, and they will gather out of His kingdom all stumbling blocks, and those who commit lawlessness, and will throw them into the furnace of fire; in that place there*

*will be weeping and gnashing of teeth. Then the
righteous will shine forth as the sun in the kingdom of their Father. He who has ears, let him hear.
(Matt. 13:36–43)*

So you see, these pivotal teen years are important for us today
in our own culture. They have always been important to God. It's
during those years our faith is tested in numerous ways. How we
make the faith of our fathers our own is a very important phase of
life. Will we bow the knee, or will we succumb to the wiles of the
enemy of our souls? It's our choice. Decisions made during these crucial years will either pay great dividends in the future or hinder our
maturity. We desire to be used by God. We want to be good seed. We
don't want to fall by the wayside and not be used by God to influence
others.

The same will hold for Joseph. Will he pass the tests ahead or
succumb to them? Would he succumb to natural temptation between
a man and a woman? Would he bow the knee to Jehovah? Would he
be pliable? Would he be moldable? Or would he rebel? Would he
blame others for the traumas that would engulf his life?

Remembering the Messianic Geneology: A Parentheses

Now, into this story, it has already grabbed our attention, we
want to know what comes next. And then the Bible just stops in
midsentence and brings us back to the red ribbon running through
Scripture from Genesis to Revelation: that of the Messianic genealogy (remember the prologue?) Why would God, through the writer,
deviate from the gripping story of Joseph's life? God doesn't want
us to forget His main purposes throughout Old Testament history:
Messianic genealogy and people of faith. So the writer steps back.
"Meanwhile, back at the ranch…" Here's the story in Genesis 38.

(Remember, Joseph was in Egypt. The other eleven sons were with Jacob in Caanan). Judah's sons were grown, so Judah set out to find a bride for the oldest son Er. Er married Tamar but was disobedient, spilling his seed on the ground. God took his life. Tamar was then given to the second son, Onan (law of Levirite marriage below). He too was similarly disobedient to God, and his life was also taken. Judah, for reasons too complicated to write here, refused to give his youngest and only son to Tamar to carry on the lineage of Judah, although Judah promised Tamar he would.

Deuteronomy describes this law.

When brothers live together and one of them dies and has no son, the wife of the deceased shall not be married outside the family to a strange man. Her husband's brother shall go in to her and take her to himself as wife and perform the duty of a husband's brother to her. It shall be that the first-born whom she bears shall assume the name of his dead brother, so that his name will not be blotted out from Israel. But if the man does not desire to take his brother's wife, then his brother's wife shall go up to the gate to the elders and say, "My husband's brother refuses to establish a name for his brother in Israel; he is not willing to perform the duty of a husband's brother to me." Then the elders of his city shall summon him and speak to him. And if he persists and says, "I do not desire to take her," then his brother's wife shall come to him in the sight of the elders, and pull his sandal off his foot and spit in his face; and she shall declare, "Thus it is done to the man who does not build up his brother's house." In Israel his name

shall be called, "The house of him whose sandal is
removed." (Deut. 25:5–10)

Years passed. Tamar was still barren, but not by her choice. According to both Hebrew and Canaanite cultures, brothers who died and didn't leave an heir were to take the brother's place and marry the widow of the brother. According to the law, if there were no other sons and the father was widowed, he could be the "seed" bearer to carry on the lineage. Tamar was denied the right to reproduce children for Judah's lineage. She took this law very seriously. She then deceived Judah, got pregnant by him, and had twin sons.

Judah was convicted of his own sin in not following the law given in the Hebrew culture. He, like his sons, had been disobedient. Tamar did the "right" thing in wanting to carry on his lineage. Judah says of her, "She is more righteous than I." (Gen. 38:26).

Judah had a change of heart during this time and, with Tamar's encouragement, began to follow Yahweh once again, after years of going his own way. Tamar is part of the family of Judah now, but he won't ever violate her again because she is his daughter-in-law. It's a complicated story, and one we don't understand in our day and age. It's a story, however, of God's mercy toward a wayward Judah. It's a story that brought him back to the mercy of God in his life. Judah experienced a change of heart.

My question here is: Why this parentheses? Why break in with the story of Judah? Because Judah was the man to whom the lineage of Christ belongs. The Old Testament is all about that lineage. But the story of Joseph is so gripping and has such meat that it has to be told in its entirety. Judah needed to be mentioned because of that red ribbon of Messianic lineage. Judah's story can't be overlooked. God hasn't forgotten about the Messiah nor his bloodline. On the contrary, He mentioned Judah to keep that part of the story going. In telling any story in the Old Testament, the side note of Judah helps keep our focus on what is important to God (Messianic bloodline) and also the line of faith as we see it unfolding in Joseph. Do you see both lines here?

Now back to the story of Joseph in Genesis 39.

How Does God Work in the Young?

It has been said, and I believe it to be true, that Christianity has always been a young people's movement. It is so in our day. Some of the largest ministries take place on high school and college campuses. Young Life, Fellowship of Christian Athletes, Campus Crusade for Christ (Cru), and Navigators are young people's movements. While we are young, it is the best time for the Lord to speak to us, to lead us, to take us through trials designed to woo us and win us to the Savior. When young and unmarried, God often gets a hold of our lives and like a GPS system, begins to "recalculate" our direction so that we more ably follow Him. Working on college campuses, we watched as God wooed and won students to Himself. He got their full attention, unfettered by family, marriage, children, jobs, and major responsibilities. God has always called the young into mission work. It's rare that His calling is later in life, although it does happen.

Joseph was no exception. He was in the teachable, young, moldable, pliable time of life. God knew He would use him later in places of authority. But there was work to be done, and it would take years to produce in Joseph what God intended. That's often the case with the young. Their minds and brains are pliable when God calls them, and in that process, He molds them, using the gifts He has given them. Joseph had a heart for God. He would soon be tested in ways he never dreamed of. Some tests would be common to most of us: family, work place, and friendship. Could this story of Joseph actually be our story as well?

God placed Joseph in Egypt because that's where He would mature him to be a man of God. Joseph could not have imagined the difficulties that would engulf his life nor what his future held. God did.

> *And He made from one man every nation of man-kind to live on all the face of the earth, having determined their appointed times and the boundaries of their habitation. (Acts 17: 26)*

The sovereignty of God is such an awesome subject that we really cannot understand it. In my estimation sovereignty is like eternity. Trying to understand either concept is too high for our minds to comprehend. We only know the Bible teaches both. These things are so beyond us that we must accept them by faith. Much of our lives revolve around that issue of faith.

Potiphar's House

We know from this verse that God placed Joseph in Egypt for *His* purposes. Did Joseph just "happen" to be sold to Potiphar? He could have been sold to any Egyptian family who had enough money to buy slaves. But whoever the Ishmaelites were, they had connections. They knew they could get more money for him if they went to the top. This young man was a prized possession. Anyone could tell by looking that he was strong and healthy. He would be usable for many years to come as a slave. God led Joseph to the house of Potiphar, who was a high-ranking military man in the armies of Pharaoh.

Potiphar and His Wife

> *Now Joseph had been taken down to Egypt; and Potiphar, an Egyptian officer of Pharaoh, the captain of the bodyguard, bought him from the*

Ishmaelites, who had taken him down there. The Lord was with Joseph, so he became a successful man. And he was in the house of his master, the Egyptian. Now his master saw that the Lord was with him and how the Lord caused all that he did to prosper in his hand. So Joseph found favor in his sight and became his personal servant; and he made him overseer over his house, and all that he owned he put in his charge. It came about that from the time he made him overseer in his house and over all that he owned, the Lord blessed the Egyptian's house on account of Joseph; thus the Lord's blessing was upon all that he owned, in the house and in the field. So he left everything he owned in Joseph's charge; and with him there he did not concern himself with anything except the food which he ate. (Gen. 39:1–6)

The Scripture will continue to emphasize that God was with Joseph and God was blessing what he touched. It doesn't say that Joseph *knew* God was with him. It simply says, "God was with him." God gave him favor in the workplace. He won accolades among his bosses and his peers. Potiphar liked him and trusted him with everything he had. That would include his wife when he wasn't there. But now he would be tested.

It came about after these events that his master's wife looked with desire at Joseph, and she said, "Lie with me." But he refused and said to his master's wife, "Behold, with me here, my master does not concern himself with anything in the house,

and he has put all that he owns in my charge.
(Gen. 39:7-8)

Joseph's hormones were raging as they do in all seventeen–year-olds. He was good looking, strong, and had a good work ethic. Whatever Potiphar said to do, he did. Wherever he said to go, he went. Potiphar's wife watched this new slave, and she was intrigued.

Day after day (we don't know how long), when Potiphar wasn't looking, there it was again. He had become uncomfortable but couldn't do anything about it. Did he want to do anything about it? Was she toying with his mind? It would be easy. No one would know. There were plenty of times when Potiphar wasn't around. I believe he was tempted as we are in the sexual arena. But each time he toyed with the thought, his mind was driven back to God and to the inner laws of the heart. He knew it was wrong. His heart told him so. Listen to these verses about how God works in our hearts to convince us of His presence, His love, and His sovereignty.

> *That which is known about God is evident within them; for* God *made it evident to them. For since the creation of the world His invisible attributes, His eternal power and divine nature, have been clearly seen, being understood through what has been made, so that they are without excuse. (Rom. 1:19–20)*

> *They* show the work of the Law written in their hearts, their conscience *bearing witness and their thoughts alternately accusing or else defending them. (Rom. 2:15)*

"But this is the covenant which I will make with the house of Israel after those days," declares the Lord, "I will put My law within them and on their heart I will write it; and I will be their God, and they shall be My people." (Jer. 31:33)

Remember, Joseph did not have the written laws of Moses yet. That was far in the future. He did not have the Ten Commandments where it says not to covet your neighbor's wife. He did not have the Bible as we know it today. What did he have? He had his heart and his conscience that told him adultery was a sin against God. In the verses above, it clearly states that God writes His law on our hearts and that we are without excuse.

Potiphar's wife was probably young as well as rich! She was rich enough that whatever she wanted she got. And so it wasn't long before she wanted something outside her marriage. And it was Joseph. Were there unwritten laws in Egypt concerning sexual sin outside marriage? We do not have archeological writings to know that. But were there laws of the heart? We know that our hearts can deceive us, and therefore, we can rationalize behavior. It amazes me in reading about and seeing stories told on TV about sexual sin, how often it occurs with a friend's spouse, right under their noses; and they really don't think they will be caught. Sometimes murders take place because of wanting what you can't have and "thinking" murder will solve the problem. Sometimes Don and I look at each other and ask the question, "Did they think they could get away with that?" But when sin is involved, a whole lot of rationalization comes with it. We literally "lose our minds."

No temptation *has overtaken you but such as is* common to man; *and God is faithful, who will* not *allow you* to *be tempted beyond what you are able, but with the* temptation *will provide the way of escape also, so that you will be able to endure it. (1 Cor. 10:13)*

The heart is *more* deceitful *than all else and* is *desperately sick; who can understand it? (Jer. 17:9)*

Temptation comes in all shapes and sizes. Temptation comes at inconvenient times. We have only to look at the temptations of Christ to know that temptation is normal, comes when least expecting it, and we must be able to deal with it head on as Christ did. Temptations came to the young mind of Joseph. What was he going to do about it?

Back home, Joseph had gotten everything he asked for. Jacob had seen to that. Would he now take what wasn't his? He could tell there was a look in the eyes of this woman every time he came close that suggested more to him than simple friendship. He knew the look. He knew the signs. Yes, she was married to his boss, but...

God Was with Him

At this point in the story, we must go where Scripture takes us. We are not told in Joseph's life like the lives of Job (Job 1:8–12) and Peter (Gospels) that Satan asked permission to sift him. But I am imagining that it could have taken place here as well. God wanted to test and train Joseph. Satan wanted him to fail. That's always the tension at play when God wants to use a person to the fullest. Remember, Satan is a watcher. He watches who God concentrates on and goes there too.

We will see throughout the story of Joseph's ups and downs and trials and traumas that God was with him. Why is this important? Because you and I must know that whatever trials come our way, no matter how severe they are, the Lord is with us. He sees. He knows.

He leads, protects, and guides. We may not always see or feel that He is with us. I am sure at times Joseph didn't feel God was even close to him. Sometimes when we go through trials, especially severe ones, we wonder where God is. He seems silent. Was He silent in Joseph's life? It appears He was.

God, the author of the Bible, wants *us* to know that as He was with Joseph every step of the way, He will be *with us* every step of the way. Through every heartache that we have, through the bumps and bruises, He is there. In Hebrews 13:5, it says that *He will never leave us nor forsake us.* At times it feels like He has left us or He is looking the other way. But these verses concerning Joseph show us, it is just the opposite of what we may be experiencing. The Lord was with Joseph. The Lord is with us, whether or not we see it, feel it, or experience it. No matter the circumstance in Joseph's life or in ours, God is with us. He may be silent, but he is not absent.

I believe that God is the worker of attitudes and morals in each of us. He places in us the willingness to do the right thing, regardless of what we have been taught. Joseph had to learn to stand on his own, not going the way of his own family along the lines of morality. There was something in the heart of Joseph, undefined as yet, that desired with his whole heart to go God's way.

The Test of Loyalty

Would he succumb to Potiphar's wife because she was ruler over him and had the right to command him to do her bidding? What was his moral compass, and how did he come by that? We have no record of Jacob teaching his sons about the love and grace of God. Did he do that? Was Rachel the one who taught him? When she became pregnant, she must have given credit to the only Source that could have made that happen. Was she a changed woman?

Did she teach her son spiritual things because God had shown her who He was? Did she have enough time with Joseph to teach him? All we know of Joseph is one phrase and that is what he said to Potiphar's wife. Listen to his words. How did he learn this?

> *Behold, with me here, my master does not concern himself with anything in the house, and he has put all that he owns in my charge. There is no one greater in this house than I, and he has withheld nothing from me except you, because you are his wife. How then could I do this great evil and sin against God? (Gen. 39:9)*

Joseph said he would not do this for two reasons: first, Potiphar was his boss and Potiphar trusted him with everything, even when he wasn't present. Therefore, he could not and would not sleep with the boss's wife. Secondly and most importantly, he would not sin against his God! Wow! How did he know that? God had put a moral compass in his heart. He had been raised knowing the God of his fathers. What little he knew was enough. God could trust his heart.

Thoughts on Sexual Sin

In Song of Solomon there is a passage that talks about our human tendencies toward sexual sin. It describes us in terms of a wall or a door. That is exactly what it says. A wall is not easily broken down. A door can be easily swung open. Each of us had a propensity toward one or the other.

> *If she is a wall,*
> *We will build on her battlements of silver;*
> *But if she is a door,*
> *We will barricade her with planks of cedar.*
> *(Song of Sol. 8:9)*

This passage is about being young when temptation comes. It is recorded about a young woman, but this can be applied to any young person. Sexual temptation is always strongest in the young. We see here that Joseph was a wall and would not cross that threshold to satisfy his hormones. Walls stand firm. They don't crumble. He passed the test. But what happened? Instead of being praised, he was falsely accused by both Potiphar and his wife and thrown in prison. Potiphar believed his wife above Joseph. Now, knowing men and women, I probably would have believed her as well—that is, until you hear all the facts. But he was a slave and she a slave owner. So who would you believe?

Often today we hear stories of men harassing and assaulting women as it is more common than vice versa. But how many times has a woman come on to a man, he rejects her, and she accuses him anyway. Often there is a rush to judgment. How do you prove what she said against what he said? We normally believe the woman in most cases. But occasionally, the shoe is on the other foot.

In the case of Joseph, she had his cloak. That was proof enough, even though Joseph actually fled the scene. Court cases take time to hear all the facts and make a rational decision. I was once on a jury on just such a case. When it was all said and done, the guy was vindicated because the accuser's facts were sketchy. It happens now, it happened then. Men have been put in prison for something they didn't do. Today, because of DNA tests, which proved their innocence, men have gone free after years of incarceration.

Hadn't Joseph followed the rules? Hadn't he done what was right? He had passed the test of obedience: he had worked hard, not for profit, but because it was the right thing to do. He had fended off his boss's wife's pursuit but he was incarcerated and had to serve his prison sentence. He had passed the test of temptation to sex but was being punished anyway. Where was God when it hurt? Where was justice? Didn't obedience count for anything? What purpose was the prison sentence? It appears God was silent once again in his hour of trial. Did he question God? I'm sure he did. Wouldn't you?

Even though we know the Lord is with us, it doesn't take away from questions of injustice that we may be feeling when wronged. We always ask, "Why are *You* doing this in my life?" Somehow, we know that God could have prevented and protected us from being wounded, and He didn't.

Psalm 105 lends insight into Joseph's story:

> *He sent a man before them,*
> *Joseph, who was sold as a slave.*
> *They afflicted his feet with fetters,*
> *He himself was laid in irons*
> *Until the time that his word came to pass,*
> The word of the Lord tested him.
> *(Psalm 105:17-19)*

The Lord Made Him Prosper

> *But* the Lord was with Joseph *and extended kindness to him, and gave him favor in the sight of the chief jailer. The chief jailer committed to Joseph's charge all the prisoners who were in the jail; so that whatever was done there, he was responsible for it. The chief jailer did not supervise anything under Joseph's charge because the Lord was with him; and whatever he did, the Lord made to prosper.* (Gen. 29:20–23)

Notice it says, "God extended kindness to him and gave him favor in the sight of the jailer." What a great statement. How does God extend kindness to us? By having others like us and recognize us for who we are and what we do. Obviously, Joseph had leadership abilities and gifts that were noticed, not only by Potiphar but now by the chief jailer. We naturally enjoy using the gifts God has given us. Others notice our abilities and the things we do well. We are usually rewarded for our strengths of character and our abilities.

He worked hard because it was the right thing to do. You don't work hard because of the pay—that's an important issue, but not the most important. Do you work hard as unto the Lord and not to men?

> *Whatever you do, do your work heartily, as for the Lord rather than for men, knowing that from the Lord you will receive the reward of the inheritance. It is the Lord Christ whom you serve. (Col. 3:23–24)*

Wounded By Christian People: Church, Organizations, and Businesses

Many of us, if we are honest, have been wounded by people we thought should be better Christians. If they had been, they wouldn't have wounded us so deeply. Pastors have had affairs with church staff, even divorced their wives, and married someone else. How deep is that wound to a wife and to her children?

Leaders in churches have wounded others, intentionally or unintentionally, and caused some to leave the church altogether. Others who stay in church may carry those wounds into the next situation.

Sometimes a wound in the workplace, not dealt with, affects the next job situation. This can happen in a secular business or a Christian church or organization. But if the wounding has been from a Christian to a Christian it can be devastating. We put a higher standard on Christians in the workplace. Christian owners, bosses, and people in authority should be held to a higher standard. But often they are so busy growing their endeavors they wound employees without a passing glance.

It has been said, "*Only Christians shoot their wounded!*" In a foxhole, when one soldier is in trouble, other soldiers will gather around and protect the wounded one. But in the church, gossip is prevalent. Satan is a divider and uses people who accuse others to divide further. Wounded people should be surrounded with caring, loving protection. Listen to the verse below.

> *Then I heard a loud voice in heaven say: "Now have come the salvation and the power and the kingdom of our God, and the authority of his Messiah. For the* accuser of our brothers and sisters, *who accuses them before our God day and night, has been hurled down. (Rev. 12:10)*

The people in our churches, that's us, need to understand that it is the power of Satan who uses us to wound our brothers and sisters. When we are wounded, we need others to surround us, encourage us, causing us to lift our hearts toward the Lord Jesus, giving us strength. Instead we often shoot our wounded, wounding them further. We say hurtful things to them or about them. These are the very people we once loved. Now we say and do things that wound them. Or they say and do things to hurt us.

It's interesting to note that in Joseph's life he was treated with more respect in Potiphar's house than in his own family. But that he was wounded in both houses is not beyond comprehension. Anytime we put our faith in our family, or in our place of business, rather than in the Lord Himself, we will get disappointed. We are human with soft hearts. Soft hearts get wounded by the people they once loved.

Joseph was no exception. Neither are we. Let's define different kinds of wounds:

Small wounds: wounds have a way of taking on a life of their own. We can be quickly wounded by something said, and it really doesn't have an impact. It comes quick, and it's over just as quick.

Deep continuous wounds: there's the wounding that happens little by little. This kind of wounding occurs over time by numerous things either said or done to you. The final wounding may appear to have happened quickly, but in actuality, it has taken a long time with many small wounds. Finally you either blow up, leave that workplace behind, and sometimes remain bitter for an extended amount of time.

Instantaneous wounds: there's the wound that happens out of the blue. It's sharp, pierces deep, has no forewarning, and simply astounds you with its pain. You are blindsided. This kind of pain lasts quite awhile with a lot of questions and few answers.

However the pain comes, it is a gaping wound until the Holy Spirit of God can get into it and heal it. We live with family so we can more easily resolve conflict over time and with help. Wounding in the workplace is one of the most devastating because often there is no closure. Unlike family or friendship wounding, where there's the possibility of counseling to repair the situation, the workplace is usually not a situation you come back to for resolution.

Men and women process wounding in the workplace very differently. If the wounding happened to a husband, son, or daughter in the workplace, the wife/mother carries the hurt differently and maybe longer than the actual person who was hurt. We are mother hens when it comes to members of our family. We are very protective. Women can get over a hurt to them personally more easily than they can concerning a person of their immediate family (spouse or child). We are mother hens who try to protect those whom we love.

My Story of Being Wounded

Remember in the last chapter I said this "Woundedness comes, not from something or someone you don't love. Woundedness comes from someone or something you *do* love." Joseph probably loved his job, albeit he was a slave. Potiphar gave him leadership and authority in his place of work. He was using his gifts of organization and leadership. In that workplace he was wounded a second time. Not because he hated his job. Just the opposite, he was good at what he did.

I want to tell you our story without belittling anyone as I believe God is sovereign and orchestrated the wound that we endured at the hands of a highly respected man.

The workplace is where careers are forged, experience is gained, and the place where we get much of our reward on this earth. It's the area that keeps us afloat financially. It's the area where our gifts are honed and matured. It can also be a place of deep woundedness when gifts are misunderstood, personalities cloud issues, and issues of opinion or direction are in opposition.

Don and I both came out of college and went into ministry. Because we were in ministry, we didn't think we would have marriage problems. How naive we were! Within twenty-four hours we started on what would be a three-year battle of the wills. Don began to ask the question, "If God made marriage, can He make it work?" He began studying Scripture on marriage and found that the Bible had a great deal to say about marriage. We left one ministry to begin another. This one centered on biblical marriage. Don and a group of men wrote material and spoke in seminars on biblical marriage principles. Our ministry flourished, and we were excited about what God was doing in our lives. All during this time we were raising a growing family of four children.

Our second "calling" for many years was church planting. We longed for a church experience that was warm and friendly and taught the Bible in simple, practical ways. We felt the church was lacking in "putting into practice" what we heard on Sunday mornings, so we established meetings in homes, called small groups or mini-churches. Our first church plant was in Dallas, and several years later, we planted the second in Little Rock. We loved the idea of starting something from scratch and watching it grow as God blessed it. Both Don and I loved being on the ground floor of churches, ministries, and anything else the Lord led us to start. We didn't realize that both of us had entrepreneurial gifts God was using to mobilize others in ministry. We have realized over many years that we are small church, small group, and small ministry-oriented people.

In the midst of these varied ministries, we were asked to work with congressional couples in the DC area, teaching about biblical marriage. We were also asked to start our third, fourth, and fifth churches there, which we did with great enthusiasm.

While in DC a major wound came out of nowhere! A very godly man, known to literally thousands, asked that we bow out of ministry with them. I literally felt a sword pierce my very being. He wanted our writing but not us!

Don was very gracious to this man. But the wound was deep and painful. It didn't make sense. We submitted and went on with our life of church planting and marriage ministry. The wound festered for about five years, and tears would flow easily and often. Sometimes I hurt so bad I could hardly breathe.

I saw Don reacting to this wound very differently than I did. Men have a way of compartmentalizing everything that goes on in their lives. Things are in boxes in their brains. They can go from one box to another, one box not necessarily affecting another. With women, our brains are wired incredibly different. What affects us in one part of our brain affects the whole. When taking care of a baby, I can still be affected by something someone says that has no bearing on the baby. I don't compartmentalize. So the wounding and the pain never seemed to go away, no matter what I was doing or thinking. Female brains seem to be a tangled up mess!

I often asked Don why the different woundings didn't affect him like they did me. We didn't have answers in those days on how our brains were wired but only to know that I felt the pain more often and more deeply than he seemed to. The men who wounded us confused me as they simply went on with life, never saying thank you, nor acknowledging our part in their ongoing ministry.

I loved teaching women, however, and decided to teach the whole Old Testament to a group of congressional wives. When I came to the story of Joseph in Genesis, it dug deep into my heart and soul. I felt if Joseph could forgive his brothers for what they had done, then I could forgive the man who wounded us. When I saw Joseph being wounded for something he wasn't guilty of, well, I connected. He had been wounded where he worked. I felt I had gone into that prison cell with Joseph. My feet were in fetters. I was shackled to my pain.

This was not the only time we had been wounded in the workplace. Another time had been when a good friend in our church planting ministry questioned Don's ability to start things and then walk away from them. At the time Don and I had not really understood how he was wired and gifted. Both of us enjoyed the ground floor of so many things. This was not only a calling but a gifting from the Lord, which we didn't understand back then. Don and I both loved getting things started and watching them grow. To put others in management after the start-up was easy for him. We were always "working ourselves out of a job."

Another period of wounding came for Don in a secular job years later. Through the first ten years of this new business he weathered some pretty big wounds but stayed 25 years, knowing he was in the position God had placed him in. It was painful, and there were more questions than answers.

Looking back on the different woundings that came for us, you would think we would grasp the Lord's dealings with us quicker. Alas, when trials would come when wounded, God asked us to "count it all joy"! You must be kidding! No one, and I mean *no one*, counts trials joy until you pass through it and look back. That's why God gives us the reminder. Trials and wounding always take us by surprise. Walking through them helps us understand God as well as our fellow man when they walk through wounding.

In chapter eight of this book you will read what happened to Joseph in prison. You will see how his life affected mine in ways I can't even begin to calculate. The white spaces of Joseph's prison years were mine as well. No other story in the Bible connected to the story of my own life as did Joseph's. It's my favorite chapter in this book. It's my favorite chapter in my own life. God is a God of the miraculous. And He is a God of mercy. He is a God of love. He knows exactly what He is doing in our lives at any given moment, and He understands the why's of it all. God is truly with us through the ups and downs of life, even when we don't see, think, or feel His presence. Sometimes, however, He speaks so loudly it would be a mistake to think any other thoughts!

A song that has meant a lot to me is concerning pain in trials is "Flawless."

Flawless
by MercyMe

Let me introduce you to amazing grace
No matter the bumps
No matter the bruises
No matter the scars
Still the truth is

The cross has made you flawless.
No matter the hurt
Or how deep the wound is
No matter the pain
Still the truth is
The cross has made you flawless

Take a breath, smile, and say
Right here right now, I'm ok
Because the cross was enough
No matter the hurt
Or how deep the wound is
No matter the pain
Still the truth is
The cross has made you flawless

Questions for Chapter 6:

1) At what age did you become a believer in Christ?

2) Were you able as a young person to learn how to share your faith? How did that happen? If not, what do you need to do now?

3) Have you or your spouse been wounded in the workplace? Have you been able to resolve it?

4) Of the two types of wounding (family, workplace), which has been the most difficult to work through? How long did it take?

5) Have you experienced a time when Christians "shoot" their wounded?

CHAPTER 7

THE WOUNDS OF FRIENDSHIP

The Test of Friendship and Betrayal

*Then it came about after these things, the cup-
bearer and the baker for the king of Egypt offended
their lord, the king of Egypt. Pharaoh was furious
with his two officials, the chief cupbearer and the
chief baker.*

*So he put them in confinement in the house of the
captain of the bodyguard, in the jail, the same
place where Joseph was imprisoned. The captain of
the bodyguard put Joseph in charge of them, and
he took care of them; and they were in confinement
for some time. Then the cupbearer and the baker
for the king of Egypt, who were confined in jail,
both had a dream the same night. (Gen. 40:1–5)*

The next test will be one of friendship for Joseph. Research has told us that for people in prison it is common for friendships to be forged very quickly. They are confined in small spaces. They eat every meal together. They have time to talk and tell their stories. Joseph, as you will note, is no exception. It is noted that many times men commit the same crimes so that they can go back into prison where life seems less complicated.

Joseph not only befriended his peers who were put in prison with him, but I believe they were put in prison for yet another test for Joseph. You see, God still had work to do in the heart of Joseph. He had now been in Egypt from age seventeen to twenty-eight. (eleven years including his prison time).

The baker and the cupbearer became his friends. Both had dreams and needed someone to tell them what the dreams meant. Joseph interpreted their dreams and predicted that the cupbearer would be exonerated and the baker would lose his life.

Notice when Joseph tells his story, *why* he wants to be free from his prison sentence, and then notice what happens. It's a God thing! There are two reasons he wants to get out. He states it. But it will actually become three reasons. At this point in his life he still believed that a "person" could help him. In this case, the man in point. See what happens.

> *"Within three more days Pharaoh will lift up your head and restore you to your office; and you will put Pharaoh's cup into his hand according to your former custom when you were his cupbearer.*
>
> *Only keep me in mind when it goes well with you, and please do me a kindness by mentioning me to Pharaoh and* get me out of this house. *For I was in fact (1) kidnapped from the land of the*

Hebrews, and even (2) here I have done nothing
that they should have put me into the dungeon."
(Gen. 40:13–15)

(numbering and emphasis mine)

In other words, Joseph told the cupbearer that when he got out
he would have the power to get Joseph out. All he had to do was put
in a good word and, voilà, Joseph would be free!

Does he still harbor issues with his brothers? *Yes.*

Does he still harbor resentment toward Potiphar and his wife?
Yes.

Is life unfair? *Yes.* He doesn't deserve this life he's in.

Verses 14 to 15 are hinge verses

> *What comes before it is resentment.*
> *What comes after it is life altering.*

He was still grappling with the injustices that befell him. He
hadn't come to any conclusions at this point in his life. When he
interpreted the dreams of the baker and cupbearer and they were
released, he asked the cupbearer to remember him so he could get
out of this prison he was in.

> *Pharaoh restored the chief cupbearer to his office,*
> *and he put the cup into Pharaoh's hand; but he*
> *hanged the chief baker, just as Joseph had inter-*
> *preted to them. Yet the chief cupbearer did*
> *not remember Joseph, but forgot him. (Gen.*
> *40:21–23)*

The man evidentially either forgot or deliberately didn't mention Joseph because he feared for his job again. We are not told the reason. It is my opinion that *God* made him forget. God was not yet finished with the molding process of Joseph for the glory of God and the salvation of his people.

When life isn't fair, know that God is a just God. He sees every injustice. He sees every tear. He hears our complaints and knows how to make things right. God will either make things right on this earth or He will tell us the reason why when are face-to-face with Him. Everything that has touched your life has first passed through God's hand. Trials are beneficial for our character maturity and so that we would have compassion for others. God is chasing after our hearts. He will not let up till He knows the work has been accomplished.

Listen to this true story of the missionary Henry Morrison (1857–1942).

After serving as a missionary for forty years in Africa, Henry Morrison became sick and had to return to America. As the great ocean liner docked in New York Harbor, there was a great crowd gathered to welcome home another passenger on that boat. Morrison watched as President Teddy Roosevelt received a grand welcome home party after his African safari.

Resentment seized Henry Morrison and he turned to God in anger. "I have come back home after all this time in service to the church, and there is no one, not even one person, here to welcome me home." Then a still, small voice came to him and said, "You're not home yet."

God sees the battle of the heart. We want accolades for service done for God and for man. It's in our DNA to long for recognition for what we've done. It's not wrong. It's human. When we don't get it, we have a tendency to place blame on people, when it's God who is actually withholding recognition for a purpose. He does what He does for a higher purpose unknown to us at the time.

The Blame Game: We All Play It

My conjecture is that Joseph did wrestle. You will know the reasoning shortly. He did question God as to why he was in Egypt at all. Was it the fault of his brothers? He was playing the what-ifs and the if-onlys.

What if my brother's hadn't done what they did? I would be home with my father and probably married to my childhood sweetheart.

If only they hadn't hated me so much.

If only the caravan of Ishmaelites hadn't happened by.

If only Potiphar's wife hadn't come on so strongly to him.

What if Potiphar had believed him instead of his wife.

What if I had gone to bed with Potiphar's wife? Would it have made a difference? I was punished anyway!

If only I wasn't a slave, people would believe me.

If only God had intervened, I wouldn't be in this mess.

Why didn't my friend remember me? What are friends for?

And why was he in prison in the first place? He hadn't committed a crime although he had been accused of attempted rape. Unjust? You bet it was unjust. Why would God have put him in a place of honor under Potiphar and his wife having access to him? What was the purpose of all this? If the brothers hadn't done what they had done and if Potiphar's wife hadn't done what she had done…

"What on earth is God doing? What have I done to warrant such animosity? What have I done? God, why are you treating me like a common criminal? *Why are you silent?* God, You could change my circumstances. What are You doing? Where are You?"

Three Injustices: Family, Work Place, and Friendship

He is now grappling with three injustices: brothers, Potiphar's wife's accusation and Potiphar actually believing her over you, and being forgotten by one whom you thought was your friend.

So now we see several tests God was asking him to pass. (Psalm 105 says that the Word of the Lord tested him.) He didn't know it, but God knew his heart and knew he needed time to process hurtful issues of family, workplace, and friendship. Joseph was just like us. He is not on a pedestal as some would have him be. He wrestled with God when there was an unjust situation and conclusions needed to be resolved. He is not above us; he is one of us. God was working on him, the same as He does us. He experienced trials, the same as us. He asked questions of God, the same as us. It's not recorded, but it's in the white space.

The Prison of Hurt

Remember again: woundedness comes, not from what we don't like but from what we love. Joseph had once again been elevated in the prison to be over prisoners. He befriended them, as people in prison often do. He also interpreted their dreams correctly and knew he was being used by God to save one of their lives. He thought that now he would be released because of the friendship he gave to another. It was another wounding that God would make him endure without answers to his questions.

Why is the story of Joseph so powerful? Is it because he was so "godly" all his life? No, it's just the opposite. He is just like you and just like me. How would I have talked to God in prison? Would I question God? How were his questions resolved? I am sure that he told God, "Okay, I am in Egypt because my brothers sold me. They hated me. Wow. I don't believe I did anything to warrant *that*, but okay, I am here. You blessed me with a good job and promotions. Then I got put in prison by doing the 'right' thing. I didn't go against You, nor did I go against my boss. Yet here I am. I was hoping the guy I befriended would get me out, but that didn't happen. Good friend he was! So now what do You want me to do? What was the purpose of giving me the interpretation of the dreams of these two men? I thought that would be worth something! What on earth are You doing in my life?"

I do not want to minimize the pain of hurt or betrayal. That kind of pain is excruciating because it stabs and bleeds. So I am not saying it isn't hard. It's very difficult. When any of us feel this kind of betrayal, it is in the pit of the stomach. We can't eat. We can't sleep. We ask questions. We play the blame game. We wrestle with God over the hurt. And we wonder if we will ever be able to make it through the pain. We also ask why a thousand times. There's no shortcut. Time goes so slowly when we are wounded. It feels like it will last forever.

Joseph would not have brought up his past to this new friend if it wasn't still bothering him. He told his whole story to one whom he thought could help him. He wanted someone, anyone, to change his circumstances. He was in prison. But he was also in the prison of his own mind. He was a slave in more ways than one. He was a slave to the prison God had put him in—the prison of hurt. Have you been there?

Family betrayal has to be one of the most excruciating things anyone of us will ever face. A sibling just doesn't like you. They want you out of their hair or even out of their life. You never dreamed that one of your siblings could ever hate you. These are the people you grew up with. They know you like no other. They were there for you and with you. They were your confidants. You played with them. You knew their secrets, and they knew yours. You looked up to them. What went wrong?

And then there's the betrayal in the work place. You thought you were doing a good job. You thought your boss really liked you. He even said he did. And then you got let go from the job for something you didn't even do or had no part of. You actually loved your job. You worked hard. You were faithful. You didn't get much appreciation but that was okay. And suddenly, it was over! Just like that!

No turning back. No thank you for a job well done. That hurt like crazy!

And then there's another excruciating pain—that of the friend you thought you had. The first hurt from your friend, you may have gotten over quickly. But the second and third time, year after year? Well, you just can't get over how easily a friend can hurt you and go on with life. Sometimes a friends' hurt can be the deepest. It's a friend you thought would stick with you through thick and thin, but then something happened. And that friend hurt you so deep you can't breathe.

> *My relatives have failed, and my intimate friends have forgotten me. (Job 19:14)*

> *My friends are my scoffers: my eye weeps to God. (Job 16:20)*

A friendship can be destroyed for any number of reasons. When someone disappoints us, we often separate further with unwanted comments or opinions. It becomes a he says-she says thing, and as we know, the process of gossip looms larger and larger until we become stunned with what the other side said or did. We must be careful to separate what wounded us from the person. Only God sees the heart of another. When we have been wounded, we literally cannot see anything good in the other person.

> *See how great a forest is set aflame by such a small fire! And the tongue is a fire, the very world of iniquity; the tongue is set among our members as that which defiles the entire body, and sets on fire the course of our life, and is set on fire by hell. For every species of beasts and birds, of reptiles*

and creatures of the sea, is tamed and has been tamed by the human race. But no one can tame the tongue; it is a restless evil and full of deadly poison. With it we bless our Lord and Father, and with it we curse men, who have been made in the likeness of God; from the same mouth come both blessing and cursing. My brethren, these things ought not to be this way. (James 3:5–10)

A perverse man spreads strife, and a slanderer separates intimate friends. (Prov. 16:28)

These verses really apply to friendship. When friendship is destroyed, it is usually through the power of the tongue. Gossip fuels the flames and spreads the venom. Words cut and bruise and wound. The wounds pierce deep. When we envision a friend, it is one who sticks closer than a brother (Prov. 18:24). We cannot go through life without friendship being spoiled by unwanted or unneeded comments. When that happens, the person we thought was our friend turns out to be a great disappointment to us.

Remember the phrase, *"Expectation is the killer of relationships."* How very right that is. When we expect someone to treat us with respect, not say hard things, and always have our back, we will get disappointed every time. As with all human beings, we are flawed people and don't always say or do the right things for someone else. When people don't come to our rescue and put in a good word for us, we get even more disappointed. Our hearts begin to break.

Sometimes through mutual conversation, the friendship can be righted. But often, unwanted comments leave us reeling and wondering if that person was ever a friend in the first place. There are those friends whom we helped to elevate to positions in the workplace, and when they get there, they stab us in the back. We say to ourselves, "I thought he was my friend! A friend wouldn't treat anyone they way he treated me!" Yes, friends disappoint.

In marriage our best friend should be our spouse. Often it's our spouse who turns on us. Our planet is riddled with marriages broken apart by words that wound beyond repair. That person was our friend; they were our counterpart. We shared life. We shared children. And now it is broken because of name calling and words spoken in anger, which we, nor they, can take back.

What do you do with wounds? C. S. Lewis wrote in his book on pain: "We can ignore even pleasure. But pain insists upon being attended to. God whispers to us in our pleasures, speaks in our conscience, but *shouts in our pains*: it is *his megaphone to rouse a deaf world*." He also wrote, "Mental pain is less dramatic than physical pain, but it is more common and also more hard to bear. The frequent attempt to conceal mental pain increases the burden: it is easier to say, 'My tooth is aching,' than to say, '*My heart is broken*.'" (The Problem of Pain)

Why was God relentless in getting Joseph's attention? I believe for two reasons: Joseph needed the process of maturing that God was doing in his life. But there was a greater purpose: that of his family's survival. We will take that issue up later on. For now, God is going to leave Joseph in prison for *two more years*. Why?

Questions for Chapter 7

1) Describe the wounds you are carrying from a broken friendship or relationship.

2) What are your emotions like when you think of good friends? How about friends that are no longer in your life?

3) Where was God when all the trials of your life occurred? How has He convinced you He is there?

CHAPTER 8

THE PRISON FLOOR

Now it happened at the end of two full years that
Pharaoh had a dream. (Gen. 41:1)

Oh my! What purpose was the two full years of waiting? And why would
God have been so specific as to say, "Two full years"? That's a long
time when you think that at any moment your friend has gone to bat
for you and you'll soon be released. When I look at Scripture, and it
says something very specific, I ask why? It could have said "a short
time later" or "after a time" or "several months passed." But it didn't.
The time frame is incredibly specific. Two full years has a lot of white
space in it.

You have to remember that with God "time" is used wisely. He
never allows something that isn't purposeful. His sovereign plan and
purpose cannot be thwarted, and He knows what He is doing in our
lives through the trials we go through. God's timing isn't usually our
timing. A question that jumps out at us in this passage is that Joseph
knew he wasn't guilty so why did he even have a prison sentence at
all? Did Joseph wrestle with God over injustices, perceived or real?

Why Two Full Years?

The chapter you are about to read is my contemplation of what might have happened in the white space of those two full years. The overarching question for me when I read the story of Joseph was this: How was God going to change an arrogant seventeen-year-old kid into a thirty-nine-year-old man who responded to his brothers with a very mature and godly statement? You will see shortly why I have spent so much time on these two years in prison. We must remember the statement to the cupbearer in the last chapter:

> "*Only keep me in mind when it goes well with you, and please do me a kindness by mentioning me to Pharaoh and* get me out of this house. *For I was in fact (1)* kidnapped *from the land of the Hebrews, and even (2) here I have* done nothing that they should have put me into the dungeon.*" (numbering and emphasis mine)

When we last encountered the cupbearer, he was being released from prison. Joseph was still in prison, both physically, emotionally, and spiritually. The reason why God left him was for another test—that of the wounds of friendship. Joseph still believed that human beings were his downfall and a human being would be his savior. So in that next two years God would do something very dramatic to Joseph that would forever change his perspective. Scripture doesn't tell us what or how God worked.

I believe Joseph's heart was changed. He gave his life over to the Lord hook, line, and sinker; do or die; sink or swim. His life was God's to do with how He saw fit. We know Joseph didn't understand the cross and who the Messiah was to be. He did know there was a Redeemer coming, One who would crush the head of Satan. That had been passed to him through the generations from Adam to

Abraham. He didn't understand what we do today. *But* he did have a relationship with Almighty God who spoke to him audibly before prison, during, and after prison.

Joseph knew He loved the Lord. And he knew the Lord loved him. That is clear for us. But, like us, there may come a time as Christians when we just give it all up and let the Lord start taking over in our lives. It is usually when the chips are down and we know we can't live the Christian life and that God must live it through us. Difficult hurts may be the catalyst that breaks us.

I remember a time in my life just like this. Oh, I wasn't in prison, but I was in a prison of my own making. I had become a believer in Christ when I was nine years old. I always had an innate desire to follow Him. I wanted to serve Him. I wanted to know Him. I tried to live the Christian life, but each year that passed was more miserable than the last. I had no idea what to do. I tried to follow the Lord in high school but was pretty miserable on and off. Then college followed with the same dissatisfaction looming over my mind. I went to church, Bible studies, youth groups, but to no avail. I was miserable inside, always looking for the next event or retreat to satisfy me and give me a boost.

The summer I graduated from college I went to work with Campus Crusade for Christ in Minnesota. The very first week I saw people who seemed so happy and fulfilled. I certainly was not experiencing that. And then Bill Bright spoke on the ministry of the Holy Spirit one night. My heart was so heavy, but as he spoke, I felt my spirit longing for the filling of His Holy Spirit.

I had tried for so long to live the Christian life, and it hadn't worked. I had invited Christ into my life, and I knew I had everything I needed with Him inside. I had all of Him, but Christ didn't have all of me. That night, on the dock of Lake Minetonka, I gave my life to Christ hook, line, and sinker, to do with me as He chose. He could send me where He wanted, give me a future mate or not, give me future children or not. I was His, and He was mine. And my life has never been the same.

You see, when I was nine, I asked Christ to come into my life. He did. He saved me. I knew I had eternal life with Him. But as I found out that night in Minnesota, I had all of Him but He had none of me. That night I relinquished my control and gave it to Him. I was putty in His hands to do with me as He wished. The freedom that brought was monumental.

My old nature is still there, but God knows and I know that He can do anything He desires with my life and its okay with me. Did He fulfill some of those dreams I gave to Him? Of course, He loves doing that for us, his children. He did bring me the man of His choice and gave me the children of His choice and the grandkids of His choice and the ministry of His choice, but they just so happen to be my choices too. He has fulfilled me in ways I never dreamed possible, given me the ministry I never thought possible, given me the family I never thought possible. It's been a wonderful ride, not without its bumps and bruises, but a wonderful life.

I believe with all my heart this is what happened to Joseph in prison. God could have taken him out through the testimony of a friend. But He didn't. Joseph was still trusting in himself and in others to fulfill him. God had to put him on his knees.

Even though Joseph didn't know the Name of Jesus, it stands to reason that if Jesus is the same yesterday (times past even before his earthly birth), today (present time), and forever (future), that when God speaks, He speaks from Trinity. His thoughts become our thoughts through the ministry of His Spirit in us. He motivates in many respects the same today as He did five thousand years ago. His character never changes. His motivations to human beings remain the same. Before in history, people may not have had the Scriptures but they still had the "Word of the Lord." This would come through stories of history past, dreams and visions, and that still small voice through our conscience that we know is not us but other than us.

Jesus the Same Yesterday, Today, and Forever

Jesus Christ is the same yesterday and today and forever. (Heb. 13:8)

Holy, holy, holy is the Lord God, the Almighty, who was and who is and who is to come. (Rev. 4:8)

I am the Lord, I do not change *(Mal. 3:6)*

It does stand to reason then that Joseph, in his thinking, would be communing with his God and that God's thoughts became his thoughts. The Holy Spirit's work would be the same for him as it is for us today. Often we get directions from the Word of God, but more often than not, God speaks to us through our minds, our consciences.

Hear, O Israel: The Lord our God, the Lord is one. Love the Lord your God with all your heart and with all your soul and with all your strength. (Deut. 6:4)

You shall love the Lord your God with all your heart, and with all your soul, and with all your strength, and with all your mind; and your neighbor as yourself. (Luke 10:27)

Joseph would not be the exception, but the norm to that rule, as we are. The Trinity is the same yesterday, today, and forever. His principles do not change with time. His dealings don't change because human nature doesn't change. God is still asking us to give Him our lives hook, line, and sinker to do with us as He chooses. It doesn't matter the era of time, the country we live in, the circumstances that surround our lives, He is the same yesterday, today, and forever.

Give Them Up to the God of All Comfort

This is what I believe happened in the white space of those two years in prison. Joseph knew that no one was coming to rescue him. It was a sobering thought. Joseph probably wrestled with God as any one of us would have had done when all our well-laid plans have gone south. He stopped wrestling, stopped asking why, stopped wanting a human being to rescue him. One night, on his knees on that cold prison cell floor, he gave it all up. "God, I am tired of carrying all this. So tired. I am exhausted trying to figure out how to get out of here. I have tried to control my circumstances. I have tried to fix it.

"You gave me a reason to get out of prison when You interpreted dreams for two friends. But my hopes have been shattered. Here I am and here I will stay as long as you want me here. I will work hard. I will prove my worth. If I die here, so be it. *I am done wrestling with You over my past. I am done begging, asking why and wallowing in pity.* If I die in prison, let me die showing how much you love me."

That prison floor became for him holy ground.

It was where he gave God his life, forever, to do with what He chose.

He stopped playing the blame game.

He stopped asking why his brothers sold him.

He stopped asking why Potiphar's wife accused him of a heinous crime.

He stopped asking why the cupbearer forgot him.

He was done.

He put his stake down and put the past behind him.

The blame game was over.

He knew God had him right where He wanted him.

And finally, it was okay with him.

The Psalm passage tells us that *"the word of the Lord tested him."*

He stopped asking to get out of this nightmare he was in.

He settled the score there in prison.

He was done.

God clearly spoke to Joseph in that prison cell. It was in that cell Joseph heard and understood the words of the Lord to put the past behind him and go into the future serving Him, being devoted solely to him. How else could he come out of that prison cell a man who could forgive like he did? Did he go in a forgiving person or come out a forgiving person? I believe he went in very differently than how he came out. You will see that shortly in his own words, his testimony, if you will.

God is not limited by the written Word. He is not limited by visions and dreams. He is not limited to just speaking to our conscious thoughts. God is not limited. But if something is a universal principle that Jesus came to fulfill and show the world what God meant by forgiveness, then that principle has always been taught, caught, and applied in every generation, no matter the means given. That's what the faith chapter is all about in Hebrews when it lists names and their acts of faith.

In the case of Joseph, he had no written Word as we do today. He had stories passed from generation to generation. Within those stories are principles behind what we now know as the written Word of God. But if God is the same yesterday (1500 BC), today (2015) and forever, then what applies to us today also applied to people throughout all human history. He also had the Holy Spirit in his heart. Listen to this passage:

In this you greatly rejoice, even though now for a little while, if necessary, you have been distressed by various trials, *so that the proof of your faith, being more precious than gold which is perishable, even though* tested by fire, *may be found to result in praise and glory and honor at the revelation of Jesus Christ; and* though you have not seen Him, you love Him, and though you do not see Him now, but believe in Him, you greatly rejoice with joy inexpressible and full of glory, *obtaining as the outcome of your faith the salvation of your souls. As to this salvation,* the prophets *who prophesied of the grace that would come to you made careful searches and inquiries, seeking to know what person or time* the Spirit of Christ within them *was indicating as He predicted the sufferings of Christ and the glories to follow. It was revealed to them that they were not serving themselves, but you, in these things which now have been announced to you through those who preached the gospel to you by the Holy Spirit sent from heaven—things into which angels long to look. (1 Pet. 1:6–12)*

Notice especially verse 11 in the above passage. This is talking about a time before Jesus ever came to earth to live among us. It was a time in Old Testament history, not New Testament. I am convinced that when the stories of the Old Testament were penned, the lessons had already been communicated for centuries, since the Garden of Eden. God has always had a plan to rescue mankind. The details have not always been evident, but the principles have always been there. When God told Abraham that his faith was accounted to him as righteousness, it is still so for us today. Sin has always been sin. Salvation has always been salvation. Forgiveness has always been forgiveness. How those terms were communicated may have taken different twists and turns, but they have always been communicated to a lost human race in desperate need of salvation, forgiveness, and wholeness.

When God convicted Joseph in that prison cell about forgiveness did He whisper into his conscience, "Look how much I have forgiven you. Are you now going to take forgiveness into your own hands and call for revenge when you have been forgiven so much?" You see, forgiveness has always been a principle of righteousness and faith. It takes faith to forgive. It takes a godly perspective to let go of our past. That's what Jesus did on the cross. He allowed Himself to take on all our hatred and our unforgiving spirit so that we could be free to forgive as He forgives. That's a wow concept in that prison cell.

Men and women of faith have always had the Holy Spirit of Christ living within them, convicting them of sin and leading them to righteousness. Always. From the Garden of Eden to the end times, He is the same yesterday, today, and forever. We are mistaken if we believe that we have more advantage than the Old Testament saints. We have the same Spirit of God giving witness to who God is and how He works. I am sure that when we meet Joseph someday and sit and talk with him, he will tell us of the same gospel that was preached to him was the same to us. He believed in the Messiah, he just didn't know His name. You see, it is all by faith. Seeing an "unseen" God, believing in Him, doing what He says, going where He leads. In that, Joseph and you and I are alike. It's faith, and nothing but faith, in a God I cannot see today anymore than Joseph could. I have never "seen" Him, yet I believe in Him. I love Him whom I cannot touch. Why? It is the Holy Spirit of Christ who bears testimony in my heart that I am a child of God.

The Prison Floor Became a Holy Place

What kind of wrestling took place on that cold stone floor of prison? He was in two kinds of prison: a prison he could see, touch, and feel, and a prison of his own making, full of the darkness of hatred, unforgiveness, and questioning his own belief system. Yes, I believe he wrestled with God over the wounds that took their toll on his life. God needed those two full years.

He too was in the ring with God. Who would win this match? Would he go down for the count? Would he need his thigh to be bruised like his father, or would he be pliable to the still, small voice of a gentle, yet demanding God?

Did Joseph ever ask what the disciples asked Jesus? I believe if he was human he did. Listen in on that conversation with Peter and Jesus.

And when He (Jesus) had spoken this, He said to him, "Follow Me!" Peter, turning around, saw the disciple whom Jesus loved following them; the one who also had leaned back on His bosom at the supper and said, "Lord, who is the one who betrays You?" So Peter seeing him said to Jesus, "Lord, and what about this man?" Jesus said to him, "If I want him to remain until I come, what is that to you? You follow Me!" (John 21:19-22)

Jesus told Peter to follow Him. Peter looked around and saw the other disciple and said, "What about him?" To which Jesus replied, "That is not your business. What I do or how I speak to someone else is My business. Your only issue is follow Me." What do you do with that? Did Joseph ever say to God, "Okay, I can forgive them. But what about them? What are *You* going to do about them? Have You convicted them? Are they sorry for what they did? Are you going to ask them to make things right?" To which God would reply, "What's that to you? I am not talking to them or about them. I am talking to you. What are *you* going to do?"

We don't want to leave this conversation with God without His confirmation that He is dealing with the *other* party. We want God to be "fair" and deal with both sides, don't we? And if we don't *see* God dealing with the other side, then we don't want to deal with our side. God simply asks us to give Him the latitude to deal where He must, in His own timing, not ours. And if we never see God dealing with the other side, well, that's still not our business. I believe Joseph got it, and bowed the knee, not in protest but in total unabated surrender. It took two years! But what a relief! What freedom. What joy was his. Now it didn't matter if he was in prison or not, he was no longer judging God, nor himself, nor others. Even though he was in prison, he was now free! Freer than he had ever been before.

The Purpose of God in Trials

In looking at what took place in Joseph's life after he was released from prison, we must back up and ask this question: how was Joseph different than that seventeen-year-old kid who was prideful and rather obnoxious? Would his time with Potiphar have changed him so dramatically? How did that prideful teenager become a thirty-nine-year-old with a perspective that was so "godly" in his responses? I venture to say it took years, it took hardship, it took wrestling, it took humbling to the point of brokenness. How else can we explain his transformation?

People usually don't change dramatically without a little help from above. This usually takes some pretty hard knocks to someone who was so filled with pride. Our personalities that we were born with, the circumstances of our family of origin, all play a huge role in who we become in the future. We have all encountered people later in life who are consumed with bitterness and blaming others for why they are the way they are. God didn't intend for Joseph to end up like his father, Jacob. Jacob, for the most part, never really changed, even after his thigh was badly bruised. He still maneuvered, lied, and blamed. His limp was always a reminder that God could and would do what it takes to humble a man. None of us are beyond that kind of severe pain.

So what was God's purpose in the betrayal of his brothers?

What was God's purpose in Potiphar's wife's accusation?

What was God's purpose in his friend's forgetfulness?

What was the purpose of two full years in prison?

My thinking here is this: Joseph was slated by God to be a redeemer to his whole family. How was that going to happen given the family he was born into? Joseph had to be taken out of his family of origin in order for God to begin the transformation project. He had to get away from his conniving father. He had to get away from his "get even" brothers. He had to get away from the dysfunction of three remaining mothers. God had things to do in Joseph's life and He needed time and space to do them so He put him in a different culture that he couldn't control. He had to learn a new language. He had to be treated as a slave with no voice on his behalf. He had to be put in a dark place with no route of escape.

God used a series of wounds in Joseph's life to bring him to his knees. First, the brothers' betrayal. Next, the accusation of sexual sin and the refusal of his boss to believe him. Third, the betrayal of a friend. These came fast and furious in the next thirteen years of his life. Just when one seemed to fade into obscurity, another came. He had no relief from the Hound of Heaven who was pursuing him with a relentless pressure to bow the knee.

God's Viewpoint

Do you see it? Joseph *had* to go to Egypt. There was a famine coming, the likes of which his generation had never seen. There was a fledgling group of nomads called Hebrews who were in much need of protection and care. The Messianic line depended on this protection. In the sovereignty of God He took one man out who would be able to save this ragtag group of people, God's chosen, and bring them to a land where they would multiply and maintain their tribal Hebrew integrity. They would be a separate but protected group of people, so that they could multiply. God had told Abraham that his offspring would become a countless group of chosen people who would one day inhabit and control the land of Canaan. This group needed time and an unhindered place of growth.

In order for God to protect them further, he needed one of their own to go to Egypt ahead of them. It was a land of wealth and prosperity. It was a land that would keep them divided without intermarriage (the Egyptians loathed anyone not of themselves). This culture would one day enslave them and treat them so badly that they would be clamoring to leave. But I get ahead of myself.

Joseph was chosen by God for a higher purpose. It wasn't about him; it was all about God and His plan. Joseph was taken to Egypt for his sake, but also for the sake of his family. God saw all the brothers and their flaws. He knew He could work with this obnoxious and prideful teenager. It would take some time. It would take some hard knocks. It would take some bumps and bruises, but he was valuable and usable material. Beneath his outward pride was a heart that just needed the softening work of the Holy Spirit.

God knew that in Joseph was the kind of heart that, softened enough, would be submissive to a Holy God. Pride is hard. It is frontal. It is repulsive. That same heart of pride can be turned into a heart of compassion and love for fellow man. God saw in Joseph a heart that was pliable, movable, bendable, and usable. If Satan had indeed asked that Joseph be sifted, then he simply was. It took years, but his heart proved that he was God's possession and could be molded into the image of His Dear Son.

We are never sifted without the authoritative permission of God. There are two examples in Scripture (Job and Peter) that show us it could happen with every leader God intends to use for the building of His kingdom on planet Earth. For most, we don't get to peek into the hidden story going on between God and Satan. Joseph was slated by God to be a leader in two different cultures: Egypt and Israel. He had to be changed from that prideful seventeen-year-old with little judgment to a ruler with great discernment. God knew just what it would take: a few trials intermingled with time. Joseph had potential, but he had to use it for good and not for selfish purposes.

Our Viewpoint

What do we do with injustice? How do we pray about it? How do we answer our critics? Is God fair? Not really. He is just. He is love. He can be harsh. Everything God does is done for a purpose: to further His Kingdom on earth. When He brings trials into our lives, it is for a purpose known to Him but may not be known to us. We ask questions, we pray, we beg, and we try to manipulate. God will not be manipulated. He purposes. He fulfills, and it's all for His glory. We don't understand. He doesn't ask us to.

What about our hearts? Are they pliable? Can God mold us into the image of His dear Son? Are we bendable? Or are we so prideful that the still, small voice of God is unrecognizable and impenetrable?

There has never been a human being on planet Earth that has not been hurt. We live in Genesis 3 where sin abounds and moral values are hidden beneath our outward pride, thinking we are more significant than we are. If we think no one has been hurt like we have been hurt, think again. Hurt brings about in us one of several reactions:

"I will never get hurt again by that person, so I will stay away from them."

"I will get them back if it's the last thing I do."

"I hope God blasts them the way I want to blast them! They have it coming!"

Then there's the other way—and I think this is why God could use Joseph—he had this other side: "God, I really don't like how things are going right now. I feel abused, left out, bewildered, hurt, and confused. But I am going to trust You with the outcome of these wounds. I bring my hurts and humiliations to your feet. Do with them what you will. I am putty in your hands. Mold me and make me what you want me to be."

It's only at the cross that we begin to see how hurt our Lord was. He was humiliated. But He took it because He loves us and wants to show us that we can do the same as we follow Him. We can't do this on our own. We must be totally submitted to a Holy God so that He can work on our pride.

Hurt laid at the feet of Jesus takes the sting away. We begin to see what God is doing in our lives. We begin to look at people from His vantage point and not our own. We see the flaws in others in right perspective. Then we see the flaws in our own personalities also in right perspective. Forgiveness is the only way to solve these issues of hurt and rejection.

I think of the Charleston shooting of nine church people in 2015. They wrestled with it but immediately forgave the guy who killed their relatives and friends. What kind of people do that? People who have been hurt. People who have experienced rejection. People whose pride has been changed to humility.

Which is more difficult? To forgive or to harbor resentment? Which takes the burden off, and which piles the burden deeper?

Why is forgiveness more difficult, but why does it result in more release?

While writing this book, the Lord once again took me to the woodshed. I told you Don and I have experienced some very deep wounds and how God dealt with me (us) through giving perspective through the avenue of time. This past year we have watched, agonized, and prayed with several of our adult children as they have experienced wounding from family members, friends, and especially the workplace. All the wounds have come from Christians. At times I have said, along with them, "God, this isn't fair!" And you know the answer to that one! God never promised that life would be fair on this planet. I was flattened anew when I realized that Jesus could have spoken those same words on the cross but He didn't. He knew there had to be suffering in order to fulfill the work of the cross.

We too must suffer with the "unfairness" of life. We must submit to the pain and bewilderment of suffering unjustly. It's the way of the cross. We don't die, but at times we sure want to. I remember watching my grown kids go through the pain of being wounded and I got in the car and shouted at the Lord, "Why would you have me write a book on wounding right now?" To which He shouted right back with, "Because this isn't theory!" And I crumbled. And I wept. And I gave it up to Him who knows the beginning from the end. I gave my precious kids to Him again for Him to do what He had to do in their lives to make them men and women of God. There is no shortcut.

Have you ever wrestled with something or someone for years with no answers? Someone hurt you, time and time again? And that someone was a very close friend or relative? Along with the disciple Peter, you just wanted to chop someone's ears off? (Garden of Gethsemane). Each time you thought of that person either a sword pierced your stomach again or you became angry all over again.

Someone got something you rightfully deserved?

Someone accused you of something you didn't do? You're still wearing that rope around your neck.

Someone got promoted for a job you worked hard for.

Someone got a raise and you didn't.

Someone got engaged to the man/woman you thought was yours.

Someone plagiarized your work and got the credit.

You went bankrupt while others gained financially.

You lost your home and bank account while others flourished.

Your ministry went downhill while others succeeded.

Your marriage dissolved in divorce. Your children have yet to recover.

During that period you prayed, you begged God, you pleaded— and nothing happened.

You accused God of being deaf, or at least it crossed your mind.

You played the blame game.

You played the what-ifs so many times:

What if he had not done what he did, you would now be happy?

What if your ministry had turned out differently, like you envisioned?

What if your boss had actually recognized your worth?

You played the if-onlys:

If only she had been more sensitive to me we would still be friends.

If only my brothers had been more sensitive to me.

If only Potiphar's wife had been content to be friends.

If only my family understood me.

If only I had not lost my position.

If only my wife understood me.

If only my husband loved me.

If only I had not been so abused.

If only I had not been bullied in school.

If only my dad had been there for me.

If only I had had a dad, or mom, or whatever.

If only my child hadn't been murdered, or killed, or maimed.

If only I had normal kids like all my friends.

If only I had more money.

If only my husband wasn't so stingy.

If only my wife would love me.

If only my boss actually knew what I did for him.

If only I could lose weight.

If only I was in better shape.

If only they had seen you in the light you see yourself, those things wouldn't have happened.

We do this all the time.

We blame others for where we are.

We blame others for how unhappy we are.

We blame others for how our life turned out.

We blame others for our lack of finances, job, or retirement.

Ultimately, we blame God because He could have come through for us or protected us, and He didn't.

If Joseph was just like us, he played the blame game. He asked the what-ifs and the if-onlys. God put a noose around his neck until he buckled from the wrestling. How do we know? The next chapter of his life will tell us this.

Giving Up Self to Find True Self

Every time we go through pain and suffering we have to go through the "giving up" of something: our concepts of who we are, our dreams, our goals, our ideas of the future. We come out of that period of suffering with less baggage for our journey. Each time it is the "losing of self" to find our true meaning. It is also the "giving up" of our former concepts of who God is to finding who He really is—the real God, the good God, the compassionate God.

Joseph *had* to be ripped from his family of origin to find out who he really was and who God was to him. He never would have left the comforts of home on his own. Joseph will learn in the future what it means to live in the "big picture" that God would give him. He will see it more fully as his brothers come and the lights go on, but for now he is finding God in the "smallness" of his circumstances in a prison cell. Later he will declare the big picture to his brothers, who will not understand. Joseph had to go to the depths of despair, give it all up, before he would fathom the scope of his own future and that of his extended family.

Trials Bring Empathy and Sympathy

Could our suffering be the very thing that brings healing to our own souls? I don't know the answer to that, but I do know that suffering brings empathy for others. When we get wounded, we more easily understand the pain that others suffer. A mother who has a special needs child will more easily understand other mothers going through the same thing. A painful divorce causes a person to be patient with another who is also going through divorce. A person who has been wounded in the workplace understands others who experience baffling wounding.

It's true that I cannot cry your tears or feel the tightness in your chest or the heartache of your soul, but because I have been wounded, I more fully understand your pain when you are wronged.

How Do You Rid Yourself of Bitterness

Somehow, into Joseph's dreams, conscious thoughts, or the still small voice of God, He must have encouraged Joseph to be thankful. Thankful that he was in prison? Yes. Thankful that his brothers had betrayed him? Yes. Thankful for how he had been treated with respect by not only Potiphar but his jailor? Yes.

> *For all things are for your sakes, so that the grace which is spreading to more and more people may cause the* giving of thanks *to abound to the glory of God. Therefore we do not lose heart, but though our outer man is decaying, yet our* inner man *is* being renewed *day by day. For* momentary, light affliction *is producing for us an eternal weight of glory far beyond all comparison, 18 while we look not at the things which are seen, but at the things which are not seen; for the things which are seen are temporal, but the things which are not seen are eternal. (2 Cor. 4:15–18)*

What does a thankful heart do for us? No matter our circumstances, no matter our trials, if we have a thankful heart, we can go through life serving others, thinking of others, and being thankful to God. When we are thankful, we rub off on others. The jailor noticed. The cupbearer noticed. I am sure his fellow prisoners noticed. It's the same with us. People want to be around us. Who wants to be around a negative-blaming person? We don't even know what to say in those circumstances so we tend to stay our distance.

God is a good and forgiving God. He is also just. He doesn't look at our past failures and hold those against us. He looks at our heart. He is quick to forgive. Am I? He is quick to restore. Am I? He knows how to motivate because we are His children. We carry His name; therefore, He treats us as sons and daughters. Can we not do the same with others who are really our brothers and sisters in the family of God? Can we look past their wounding us to the wounds they carry from their past? Can we have compassion on them?

What are the wounds you are carrying around? Do these wounds stem from childhood trauma: bullying; unstable home life; parent's traumatic marriage or divorce; unreasonable father; hurt from best friends; wounds from a parent who were physical, emotional, or both? Have there been wounds recently in your life, from friends, from your marriage, from the workplace?

You won't ever feel thankful for wounds and hurts in your life. This is a matter of choice, not feelings. Make a list of your wounds that have never been resolved. As you list those wounds that have been piled one upon another for years, begin thanking God, first of all that He brought you through those wounds. Then begin thanking Him that in being wounded, you now understand others who are wounded. When you begin thanking God for the wound itself, it will begin to relieve you of the pain and trauma you have endured. God wants you to know, as He was with Joseph in his wounding, He is and has been with you in yours. He walks alongside you, giving perspective, wisdom, and kindness toward others.

Thanksgiving is mandatory if you want to move past your hurts into joy. Isn't joy what we most long for? We long for peace. We long for purpose. We long for perspective from the wounding. Lay your wounds at His feet. Let Him deal with them in the gentle and gracious way only God can do. It may be years from now when you have an ah-ha moment as to the why's of your wounds. Wait for it; it will come.

Thanksgiving: God's Antidote for Healing

And we know that God causes all things to work together for good to those who love God, to those who are called according to His purpose. (Rom. 8:28)

Whatever you do in word or deed, do all in the name of the Lord Jesus, giving thanks *through Him to God the Father. (Col. 3:17)*

In everything give thanks; *for this is God's will for you in Christ Jesus. (1 Thess. 5:18)*

That verse says "in all things" not "for all things." You and I can be thankful *in* our circumstances although we don't fully understand the why's of what is taking place. We may not be thankful for the situation, but we can be thankful that God is working *all* things for our good.

Praise the Lord!
Oh give thanks *to the Lord, for He is good;*
For His lovingkindness is everlasting.
(Ps. 106:1)
The Lord is my strength and my shield;
My heart trusts in Him, and I am helped;
Therefore my heart exults,
And with my song I shall thank Him.
(Ps. 28:7)
And in that day you will say,
"Give thanks *to the Lord, call on His name.*
Make known His deeds among the peoples;
Make them remember that His name is exalted."
(Isa. 12:4)

There are a myriad of verses throughout the Bible on being thankful. A thankful heart is God's heart. As you read the next chapter of Joseph's life, you will see why I have spent so much time on his prison sentence. Something actually happened in his life that was life altering. As we read going forward, remember to think about the past. What happens in our past determines what our future will look like as well. We are not a product of our circumstances so much as we are a product of our attitude and heart in any given instance.

If Joseph could have been released from prison and not spent "those two full years," I do not believe we would have the same story that has been told for millennia. Those two years were crucial to all God did in his life. Without them the next fourteen years would have looked very different. Because of those two full years, he looked at life very differently. He chose to see God's hand in everything he did. He chose to see that God had orchestrated every detail of the pain and hurt that he had gone through or would go through in the future. He was now putty in the hand of an Almighty God. He knew it, and God knew it.

There is a portion of the film *The Mission* (1986) in which a Catholic slave trader becomes a priest. But in his heart he carried a huge burden of his past conduct toward the people to whom he is now supposed to minister. His sin was so burdensome that he actually did penance by putting a huge rope basket around his neck, filled it with pots and pans, making it very heavy, and proceeded to climb a cliff to the waiting people and his new home. He knew he deserved to be killed and knew it might happen when he reached the top. Several times the weight was so heavy that he fell back down the cliff. Each time he picked up his burden and inched forward once again. Finally reaching the top, he saw the people running at him with knives. He faced them, knowing he deserved what was coming. But instead, with their knives, they cut his burdensome pack off his back. He fell to his knees with tear-soaked face and sobbed. The men enfolded him with their arms of love. He was forgiven. From then on he was free, free to live among them, free to minister to them, free to experience joy!

I think of my life and that of Joseph when I see that story. We carry such a heavy sack of wounds around our necks, almost strangling us. Our sins are tangled with the wounds of others. Only God can cut the ropes that bind us to that burden we carry. He wants us to be free to live, free to minister, free of the pain we carry so carefully up our cliffs of life. We feel if we do enough penance, our sin and our wounds will drop from us. No, God cuts them from us when we give them up to Him and lay them at His feet.

Can you give your hurts up to Him? Will you let Him cut that burden from around your neck that's literally chocking you? He is the only One who can do that. He is the only One who can give us freedom. God rewards us when we give hurts and trials and wounds to Him. We lay them at His feet for Him to deal with, both with us and those who have wounded us. He knows how to redeem; we do not. He knows how to forgive; we do not. He knows how to motivate; we do not. He sees not only your heart, but the heart of those who have wounded you.

Trials: Heaven's Gate to Reward

Second Timothy talks about those who persevere through trials: all who came before us, all who are going through trials now, and all who will come after us. God is in the business of reward. He longs for us to come through our trials a more godly person than when we went in. Trials are heaven's gate to reward.

> *In the future there is laid up for me the* crown of righteousness, *which the Lord, the righteous Judge, will award to me on that day; and not only to me, but also to all who have loved His appearing. (2 Tim. 4:8)*

> *Blessed is a man who* perseveres *under trial; for once he has been approved, he will receive the* crown of life *which the Lord has promised to those who love Him. (James 1:12)*

160

Questions for Chapter 8

1) Describe the wounds you carry that are weighing you down.

2) Have you given your life to the Lord hook, line, and sinker to do with what He chooses?

3) Have you forgiven those who have wounded you? (Forgiven doesn't mean forgotten. It means you have given them to God.)

CHAPTER 9

FROM THE PRISON TO THE THRONE

Finally, *after two full years in prison*, the cupbearer remembered. Did he have amnesia? Was he too busy getting his own life and job back? No, God was in this whole thing and this whole two-year process. God took Joseph off the mind of the cupbearer because He wasn't finished with him. Remember that to God, time is not a problem if there is something that had to be done.

Now we come to the next chapter of Joseph's life. God had dealt graciously with Joseph in prison. He had gained much in the way of inward maturity. It appears that he was ready for God to use him in a much more significant way.

Pharaoh had two dreams, and no one could interpret them. The cupbearer heard of Pharaoh's dreams and how perplexed Pharaoh was. Then he remembered an unusual man in prison who befriended him and interpreted his own dream. He had been so busy with his job that he almost forgot about Joseph. He would see what he could do.

Let's stop and analyze. What if Joseph had not finished wrestling but had been promoted quickly to power and then his brothers had come? What would he have done? He would have had the authority to put them in prison and probably would have done just that. If he had not put the past behind him and forgiven his brothers for their betrayal what would be his thought pattern? Did he forgive Potiphar and his wife for the unjust prison sentence? Was he still asking why? Was he still blaming people for his misery? You see, he was still wanting "out."

My theory is that it was *in* the full two years where he languished in prison that he gave it all up to God. He stopped blaming his brothers for his plight and instead bowed the knee to Almighty God to do with him as He chose. *This two-year period was the "hinge" in his life.* It was the settling with God that God was in charge. It was understanding that God was and is sovereign and He can do whatever He pleases, whenever He pleases, with whomever He pleases. It was the hinge time in his life when he turned it all over to God and was free for the first time in his life to really be who God created him to be. Joseph was a good man. God wanted to make him a great man. He was a kind man. God wanted to make him a compassionate man. He had leadership skills. God wanted to use those skills for a purpose yet unknown to him.

You see, Pharaoh didn't dream two years previous *because Joseph wasn't ready to be used for* God's *purposes.* The two full years in prison was the "hinge" in his life. Before that, the story was all about him. After those two years, the story will be about God—His sovereignty, His purposes, His plan, His strategy, and His glory.

My Story Once Again: My Holy Prison Floor

I have had two dramatic changes in my life. One, I told you about happened after college when I first understood the ministry of the Holy Spirit in my life. That was when I gave my life over to the Lord—hook, line, and sinker to do with me what He chose for me. It was a dramatic change when I realized that I wasn't in control any more but God was. This was an ongoing process of renewal for the rest of my life. My worldview continues to change. My mission changed. My thought patterns changed. Notice, I said *process*. I didn't become someone else. I started to become who God created me to be. Do I still struggle sometimes? Yes, but it's different. I don't struggle with who God is, nor that He is sovereign in my life. I struggle with changes I still want to see happen in my life.

The next dramatic change happened to me after the woundedness in the workplace that I mentioned in chapter 7 of this book. I began to study and put into practice the incredible story of Joseph. I stopped blaming someone else for the circumstances I found myself in. I began to look at life from God's perspective, the same way Joseph did. I began to see that Don and I were not ousted from the job we loved because God hated us. We were right in the center of God's will. Along with Joseph, I knew that God had done this, not man. I also knew that God still had His hand upon our lives to do with us how He chose—where, when and how. I bowed the knee once again to be pliable in the hands of an almighty, all-knowing, all-purposeful God. I have been changed to this very day, knowing that God has my back. He loves me and has allowed wounds to come for my benefit. I can identify with others who are experiencing wounds, either from what happened to them or at their own hands.

I have also gained perspective on how I blame God for those wounds that come my way. I wouldn't overtly say God was to blame, but by my actions I blamed God for not coming through for me when I felt I needed Him most. I'm like Adam, blaming the woman *you* gave me (Gen. 3). I want God to do *my* bidding; and all the time He was working on me, humbling me, showing me my own anger, entitlement, and neediness.

Here is a song that has captured my submission to a Holy God.

"Hungry, I come to You for I know You satisfy. I am empty, but I know Your love does not run dry. So, I wait for you, Oh I wait for you. I'm falling on my knees, offering all of me. Jesus, You're all this heart is living for. Broken, I run to you, for Your arms are open wide. I am weary, but I know Your touch restores my life. You're all this heart is living for."*

When we give our wounds to Him, He heals in his timing, not ours. He is able to take on our wounds because that's exactly what He did at the cross. He died for all our sins, but He also died for all our wounds. By His stripes we are healed. I cannot heal myself. Only He can do that. I cannot take away the pain. Only He can do that. That's why He wants us to come to Him, lay the wounds at His feet, so that we can see them for what they are.

During my time of unrest and pain, Don kept reminding me that the people who hurt us were not our enemies. Satan is our enemy who wants us to believe that people are our problem instead of him. Ephesians 6:12 took on new meaning concerning flesh and blood (people).

For our struggle is not against flesh and blood, but against the rulers, against the powers, against the world forces of this darkness, against the spiritual forces of wickedness in the heavenly places. (Eph. 6:12)

When I gave God my wounds He took them. And guess what? The pain began to subside. It took more time than I had anticipated, but I no longer looked at my situation with pain. I looked at it with perspective, His perspective. He is amazing! I could see His people with His eyes and heart. God has redeemed, not only Don and me, but the very people who wounded us. God is the One who is working in all our lives to bring glory to Him. When we believe that others are trying to destroy us, we get into Satan's camp. We are never happy there. We think if they would just apologize or restore us to our former position (glory) then everything would be okay. We so want glory for ourselves.

When we blame others for what we are experiencing we are in essence destroying ourselves from the inside out. It took time for all this to settle in my mind and heart and to realize that God only wants what is best for us, individually and corporately. Looking back, it would not have been good for us to stay in that position. Others needed to be elevated so that God's Kingdom work would continue. We will never know this side of heaven all the "why's" of our lives. Only that He is in control, we are not. He sees the beginning from the end. He knows what He is doing while we simply do not.

Don and I have been restored to our former friends. We communicate. We honor one another. We rejoice in what God is doing on all sides. Only God can do that.

I believe that's the same story in the life of Joseph. He gave it all up and bowed the knee, right there in that prison cell, knowing he may be there until he died. God had been with him, he knew that. But now he belonged to God. Big difference. He would follow God even though it was in the confines of the prison walls. It doesn't say this, there is white space here, but I believe this took place because of what happened in the next chapter of his life.

Are you with me? Hang on because you are going to see why those two years were so pivotal in his life. I too had a change of heart in the five years between the wounding and the beginning of the healing. Those were "my full years" when God raked me over the coals, asked me to trust Him, and I gave it all up to Him who judges righteously. That period became a "hinge" for me.

Joseph had a change that was going to produce fruit for eternity, the likes of which he (and we) will be astounded. He will not react as his human nature told him to. He would react supernaturally. Why? Because he was a changed man. *The prison had become to him holy ground.* It was where he became humble in his heart. We will see shortly that manifestation in his life. He will actually share his testimony with the reader. Are you excited to see that?

God knows exactly what He is doing in a life that is committed to Him. Hurt may be necessary for us to relinquish our pride and humbly walk where He leads us. It's not about us. It's all about Him and His glory. Am I willing at any moment to follow Him, even though the road might be painful? Now back to the story.

Pharoah's Dreams and the Miracle That Takes Place

Then Pharaoh sent and called for Joseph, and they hurriedly brought him out of the dungeon; and when he had shaved himself and changed his clothes, he came to Pharaoh. Pharaoh said to Joseph, "I have had a dream, but no one can interpret it; and I have heard it said about you, that when you hear a dream you can interpret it." Joseph then answered Pharaoh, saying, "It is not in me; God (Elohim) will give Pharaoh a favorable answer." So Pharaoh spoke to Joseph, "In my dream, behold, I was standing on the bank of the Nile; and behold, seven cows, fat and sleek came up out of the Nile, and they grazed in the marsh grass. Lo, seven other cows came up after them, poor and very ugly and gaunt, such as I had never seen for ugliness in all the land of Egypt; and the lean and ugly cows ate up the first seven fat cows. Yet when they had devoured them, it could not be detected that they had devoured them, for they were just as ugly as before. Then I awoke. I saw also in my dream, and behold, seven ears, full and good, came up on a single stalk; and lo, seven ears, withered, thin, and scorched by the east wind, sprouted up after them; and the thin ears swallowed the seven good ears. Then I told it to the magicians, but there was no one who could explain it to me." Now Joseph said to Pharaoh, "Pharaoh's dreams are one and the same; God (Elohim) has told to Pharaoh what He is about to do. The seven good cows are seven years; and the seven good ears are seven years; the dreams are one and the same. The seven lean and ugly cows that came up after them are seven years, and the seven thin ears scorched by the east wind will be seven years of famine. It is as I have spoken to Pharaoh: God (Elohim) has shown to Pharaoh what He is about to do. Behold, seven years of great abundance are coming in all the land of Egypt; and after them seven years of famine will come, and all the abundance will be forgotten in the land of Egypt, and the famine will ravage the land. So the abundance will be unknown in the land because of that subsequent famine; for it will be very severe. (Gen. 41:14–31)

Joseph was put to the test of interpreting the dreams of Pharaoh—fat/lean cows and fat/lean corn stalks. In both dreams the skinny cows and skinny ears of corn ate up the fat ones. Strange dreams, huh? He told Pharaoh what to do. He, Joseph, told Pharaoh what to do! He told the king of Egypt what was going to happen and what to do about it! He made it plain to Pharaoh that Elohim (maker of heaven and earth) was the One who was in control and only Elohim could interpret the dreams.

It is interesting that when a pagan came to saving faith in the God of the Hebrews, it was by the name Elohim, maker of heaven and earth. The Egyptians worshipped many gods. Joseph is here witnessing to Pharaoh about Elohim (vs. 16). Pharaoh actually acknowledged that Joseph's God, Elohim, was the giver of these dreams and the One who would fulfill them (see vs. 39 below).

Remember that earlier in Joseph's life he too had a couple of dreams. When he told the dreams to his brothers the dreams were not interpreted. The interpretation of his dreams was yet to be fulfilled. Did Joseph remember that he too had dreams? But nothing came of his dreams. Why then is Joseph so sure that the Pharaoh's dreams are from God? This king probably didn't even know God. Can God speak to a nonbeliever? The answer here is a resounding yes! He can speak through whomever He chooses and whenever He chooses.

The Elevation of Joseph

> *Then Pharaoh said to his servants, "Can we find a man like this, in whom is a divine spirit?" So Pharaoh said to Joseph, "Since* God (Elohim) *has informed you of all this, there is no one so discerning and wise as you are. You shall be over my house, and according to your command all my people shall do homage; only in the throne I will be greater than you." Pharaoh said to Joseph, "See, I have set you over all the land of Egypt." Then Pharaoh took off his signet ring from his hand and put it on Joseph's hand, and clothed him in garments of fine*

linen and put the gold necklace around his neck. He had him ride in his second chariot; and they proclaimed before him, "Bow the knee!" And he set him over all the land of Egypt. Moreover, Pharaoh said to Joseph, "Though I am Pharaoh, yet without your permission no one shall raise his hand or foot in all the land of Egypt."(Gen. 41:38-44)

Still a Young Man

Now Joseph was thirty years old when he stood before Pharaoh, king of Egypt. (Gen. 41:45)

Joseph was released from prison and put second in command at age thirty. Why? Because there was coming a famine so severe that it would not only affect Egypt, it would affect surrounding nations as well. It would affect his own family. Joseph didn't know that. God did.

What would it be like to have been incarcerated for years for a crime that you didn't commit? Humiliating to say the least. What would it be like for the president of the United States to pardon you and wipe clean the crime slate? And then what would it be like to be elevated at the same time to vice president? That had to be a wow moment for Joseph. His head must have been reeling at all that was taking place so rapidly. And to boot he was only thirty years old. Such a change in life could only be spoken of as a miracle.

This miracle could only correspond to others like Paul being in prison. There was an earthquake, the chains fell off, and he walked out a free man. That's just what happened. There were dreams from the king, Joseph unlocked the mystery, the chains fell off, and Joseph was a free man. But unlike the apostle Paul, Joseph was elevated to a political position of leadership unlike any other story in the Bible. Miraculous? You bet it was!

Joseph's New Name

> *Then Pharaoh named Joseph Zaphenath-paneah;*
> *and he gave him Asenath, the daughter of Potiphera*
> *priest of On, as his wife. And Joseph went forth*
> *over the land of Egypt. Gen. 41:46*

These two names of Joseph and his wife are very interesting. Zaphenath-paneah and Asenath rhyme and are melodic. Finding adequate definitions has been difficult. In one definition, "nath" means "belonging to the goddess Neit." Asenath would belong to her pagan priestly father and his gods.

Other commentators give the meaning of Zaphenath as "the man to whom mysteries are revealed, one who reveals mysteries," "a finder of mysteries," "a revealer of secrets." In another Bible translation, Joseph's new name means "God speaks and lives." Remember, it is Pharaoh who gives Joseph a new name. His name would have been significant in meaning. He was a revealer of mysteries. He was a man in whom God speaks and lives. Pharaoh recognizes the Elomim of Joseph. Very interesting!

Was Asenath a pagan woman? Yes. But did she stay pagan? We are not told, but living with Joseph after his life change had to influence her life as well. I believe that she watched this man of faith and fell in love with Joseph's God. She will later join him in his family of Israelites. Joseph would always straddle two loyalties, his Hebrew family and his Egyptian family, as he ruled under Pharaoh's authority. His children would always be half Egyptian and half Hebrew. I believe at this time, however, that in and out of the home they would have spoken only Egyptian. There was absolutely no reason to identify as Hebrews in public. Joseph worshipped his God in private, and that is obvious from his statements later to his brothers. But outwardly, his customs, language, and children would have been Egyptian.

It is interesting that later we will read that Egyptians didn't eat with foreigners. If they didn't eat at the same table it is likely that they did not intermarry with foreigners. This comment is very important to grasp, and I will deal with this later in the story. Joseph had been in Egypt for thirteen years when he stood before Pharaoh, became his vice chancellor, and received a wife as a gift from Pharaoh's hand. Obviously Asenath would have been from one of the ruling and upper class families. Because Egypt worshipped many gods, the priesthood would have been very prominent and exalted. Joseph, as an interpreter of the dreams of the highest man in the kingdom, became an exception to the rule of marriage within the Egyptian culture.

Pharaoh would have never given an Egyptian woman to a foreigner without a purpose. Joseph had interpreted the king's dreams. The fulfillment was yet to come, but Pharaoh obviously believed they would come to pass exactly as Joseph had predicted. In response, he gave Joseph a very costly gift. Joseph would have never rejected this gift. Would his Egyptian wife be able to eat at the same table? I am assuming so. We will encounter the practice of Egyptians eating separately later in the story.

(Hang on to another thought: why Egypt? Why did God send Joseph to Egypt? Is there an answer? Yes, there was a reason he was sent to Egypt and not some other country.)

When he interpreted the dreams there were fourteen years to come, prophetically, seven good years and seven lean years. It was during the first seven years of plenty that he married Asenath and had two sons, so twenty years had come and gone since leaving his home in Canaan.

Joseph as Vice Chancellor

When he was released from prison he began his next job under Pharaoh. He was placed in a position he could never have imagined. He was second in command. Pharaoh never made a decision apart from Joseph. He conferred on him all matters of importance to the economic survival of Egypt. Of course, Egyptian was the only language spoken, in and out of his home. He was already proficient in the language, having learned under Potiphar and only spoken Egyptian in prison. He had done his homework on how to survive a famine. God had been his teacher. His mind was sharp. His calculations correct. Yes, Egypt would survive under the tutelage of Joseph.

Joseph had such authority that had he asked Pharaoh, he could have gone back to his family and gotten a wife from among his people. His grandfather Isaac had done that. His father, Jacob, had done that. He knew the stories. Why hadn't he?

Because he had put the past behind him those two years in prison, he accepted Asenath as a gift from Pharaoh and a gift from God. God loved the Egyptian people and so did he. They were the ones who had blessed him in his new home and new life. He would unite with them and go on. He wasn't wallowing in the past. He loved his new position and his new life. God was good, and life was good.

Positions of Leadership

In America we have the tendency to place men and women in leadership positions because they are good orators. Leaders need to be tested in similar ways as Joseph. How many speakers who are young can sway a crowd? They are placed in positions of leadership. And they don't know what to do. They may falter. They often fail. The government is strewn with leaders who may be very good speakers but who know nothing of how to run a country. Leadership takes time to develop properly. It often takes a couple "failures" along the way so that the person is humbled and doesn't take credit for the good that occurs in his life.

We look at young pastors who are gifted in oratory. We place them in positions of leadership only to find out later they were not ready for the job. Some have even left the faith when the going got tougher than they assumed it would. Affairs are all too common among those who have been put in leadership without the proper protecting boards around them who will not tell them what they want to hear, but will in fact, tell them what they *don't* want to hear. The church is strewn with examples of young leaders who went astray, who were not vetted, and who gathered around them "yes" men. Accolades tend to puff up, and they begin to think more highly of themselves than they ought.

God knew what He was doing in the life and heart of Joseph. He had great potential as a teenager. But he had some rough edges that needed to be chipped and sanded. Part of the process that we call maturing is simply being put in positions of compromise in order to test what is in the heart. This purposefully happened under Potiphar. Joseph had to be tested. Would he succumb to sexual sin, which is a temptation of men the world over? It usually happens in young men but can happen at any age, when the guard is down and secrecy is paramount. It is interesting to me that when people (both men and women) fall to temptation it is with the idea that it will never come out in the open. How wrong they are. "Your sin will find you out."

But if you will not do so, behold, you have sinned against the Lord, and be sure your sin will find you out. (Num. 32:23)

Therefore do not fear them, for there is nothing concealed that will not be revealed, or hidden that will not be known. (Matt. 10:26)

But there is nothing covered up that will not be revealed, *and hidden that will not be known.* *(Luke 12:2)*

My husband has been a marriage counselor all our married life. He has told me stories of "needy" women who have come on to him when he was younger. He always followed the mandate to have someone else present when counseling the opposite sex. The door was open, and another person was outside to intervene if necessary. It didn't happen often, thank goodness, but that has often been the downfall of a pastor or counselor or businessman who thinks himself invulnerable to temptation.

We put people in leadership positions who have not been tested. It's a simple rule: accountability to other people is a necessity. If it's a church, the pastor needs elders who are not "yes" men. If it's a business, the owner needs people who will tell them the hard truths and not just tell them how wonderful they are. Leaders will gather around them discerning people in different areas of strength and will listen to them.

It took thirteen years for Joseph to be tested and his heart revealed. During the testing periods he was placed in leadership, but it was always under an older person. He didn't have authority to make decisions without the older person approving or disapproving. These were good tests, and Joseph passed. However, that last one, the one that lasted "two full years" was probably the toughest. And it was after this test that God knew Joseph was ready to take on the responsibility of an entire country.

The Elevation of Joseph

Can you imagine a modern-day scenario that would play out like this story? I can't. Positions of leadership are not usually given to incarcerated men, let alone men who are only thirty years old. But here was an individual who was elevated because he did a huge favor for the king of Egypt. It was knowledge that manifested itself in the interpretation of two strange dreams. We don't understand the minds of men of history, nor what makes them tick. We only know from the Bible that such men existed and their evaluations were paramount. If that king wanted you dead (the baker), then you died. If he wanted you elevated, then you were. But we also know that God changes and motivates men's minds to do what He desires as well.

> *The kings heart is like channels of water in the hand of the Lord; He turns it wherever He wishes. (Prov. 21:1)*

When Joseph was elevated and married an Egyptian woman, he was putty in the hands of Elohim, Creator of all things. He was blessed. He was a happy man. Did Joseph tell his wife about his past, his family, His brothers, and his mother's death, and the birth of his younger brother, Benjamin? Did he tell her about all the years since he was torn from his family? Did he talk about the God (Elohim) of the Hebrews so that she could understand? We have no record of any of this but do married people talk? Do they talk about their past? Do they talk about their dreams for the future? If he was normal, he did. And she responded. Of this I am certain.

He was a humble and compassionate leader. He stood with His Lord, no matter the circumstance. Pharaoh saw his stability. He saw his love for his God. I am convinced that Pharaoh talked to Joseph about his faith. We're not sure where he stood with this God of the Hebrews because Scripture is silent. We do know Pharaoh respected Joseph and his God to the utmost. Later he was willing to give Joseph the best land in Egypt for his extended family. I am sure Joseph wasn't silent about his faith. It is my opinion that Pharaoh and Joseph became "brothers in the faith." It is not a stretch of the imagination.

Pharaoh does "nothing" without conferring with Joseph. What man does that if he thinks Joseph is a "religious nut"? Hang onto that thought. What man of faith, ever in history, kept his faith to himself? None. All men and women of faith wore it on their shirtsleeves for all to see. Death came to many because of their vocalizing their faith. Joseph was no exception.

Questions for Chapter 9

1) Do you have a time in your life that you would describe as a "hinge"?

2) Describe the before and after of that hinge.

3) Why is time and testing a huge factor in developing leadership skills?

4) Why would God reveal private sins?

5) Can you keep silent about your own faith? Why or why not?

CHAPTER 10

THE STORY IS IN THE NAMES

What's in a Name?

Let's pause here to talk once more about names. Remember that Leah named her sons four names that told her story, her testimony. By the time her fourth son was born, she had a life change. She determined to praise God instead of feeling sorry for herself. Her testimony is in the names of her sons. Her conversion and change of life took place with the birth of Judah.

Now we come to the naming of Joseph's two sons. Grab onto the meaning of the names. Joseph's testimony is indeed in the naming of his two sons, just like Leah's testimony is in naming her sons.

The seven years of plenty had taken place and *during* that time two sons were born to Joseph (Zephenath) and Asenath. If you don't get the meaning, you don't know what happened *before* they were born. Change had already occurred. When did it occur? Before he was married and had sons.

The only time that could possibly have happened was *after* he told the cupbearer about his life and asked to be remembered and *before* he was released from prison, during those "full two years." *The*

179

naming of his sons was *his testimony* in a nutshell. Very simple, very life altering, and sustaining. That's what all testimonies are: we have a "before," a "during," and an "after."

His sons' names are the "hinge" from his past to his future.

The Healing Name of Manasseh

> *Now before the year of famine came, two sons were born to Joseph, whom Asenath, the daughter of Potiphera, priest of On, bore to him. Joseph named the firstborn Manasseh, "For," he said, "God has made me forget the pain of my father's household." (Gen. 41:50–51)*

When Joseph's wife became pregnant, they talked about names as all parents do. The names he gave his sons were Hebrew names. If they had Egyptian names, we are not told. What name was on the lips of Joseph for his firstborn and why?

Manasseh, "God has made me forget the pain of my father's household." That's a wow name! What does it mean? Forget? Not on your life. He didn't have spiritual amnesia. Who could forget that one of your brothers wanted you dead? Who could forget that ten of your brothers actually sold you for money? Who in their right mind forgets that kind of pain? No one. Not Joseph, not you, not me. Deep pain is never forgotten. Oh, it may weaken over time, but it's *never* forgotten.

So what is the deeper meaning of that name? It means *forgive*! "I have forgiven my brothers, every single one of them as the memory has been played over and over in my mind for fourteen plus years." Have you ever struggled over a pain so deep that it has altered your whole life? No, you don't forget. The only way for the pain to lessen is to give it up to the God of the universe who sees and hears and understands that kind of pain. God's timetable is usually not ours. God does make things right, but patiently and in His timing. We want justice yesterday. He waits. He is patient. He understands the human heart and knows how to make us pliable. Notice: in Joseph's life how many years were between the first wounding and this chapter? Thirteen years of relentless pain with absolutely no answers from God. God appeared silent until Joseph gave it all up to Him in prison.

In prison Joseph put his stake down. "*I am done.*" Done with the what-ifs and the if-onlys. Done with the blame game. Done with feeling sorry for myself. Done with the injustice. Done with the pain. "*I'm done.*"

He didn't forget. He *chose* to put it away. Joseph felt free in prison even though he was shackled. Joseph felt free now that he had a son, and he named him Manasseh as a *reminder* for the rest of his life that that chapter of grieving was over and done. Manasseh will forever say to him, "Don't go there, don't go back, don't rehash the past. Your stake was put down in prison. Don't pick it back up, now or ever!" Every time he spoke the name, Manasseh, he was reminded. Every time he kissed his cheek, he was reminded. Every time he played with Manasseh, he was reminded. The past was past. *Manasseh! I'm done!*

Wouldn't it be great if all of us had a child whose very name reminded us of our submission to a Holy God? And every time we spoke that name it was as though God Himself was speaking to us?

The Equally Powerful Name of Ephraiam

He named the second Ephraim, "For," he said, "God has made me fruitful in the land of my affliction." (Gen. 41:52)

Pregnancy came again for this royal couple. Again they talked of names. Because Manasseh meant so much, this son's name should also mean much. And one night it came to him. God had blessed him in Egypt. He had been elevated to a position of leadership that only God could have given. God had blessed him with a wonderful wife and young son. He was given free rein to plan for the future coming economic downturn. He would be able to spare Egypt from collapse and maybe help other countries along the way. He loved his life, and he worked diligently and hard because God was the one he was working for, not Pharaoh. Oh, he loved Pharaoh. He honored him. He was his friend and companion. He was blessed. Egypt was his blessing, and he thanked God for all that had happened to get him there, even the prison sentence, even the injustice of his brothers. Yes, he saw God's hand on his life in the past to bring him to his present blessings.

So the name that was fitting was *Ephraim*, which means "God has blessed me, made me fruitful. I look to the future." In other words, "The past is the past. The future is bright. God is good. I am a happy man. I am fulfilled. I can go on." What a freeing name. No burdens, no black clouds hanging over his head, no past chocking tight around the neck, no churning stomachs, no begging God to change things. The freedom of the future!

This is how I know he wrestled with God in prison. When he got out, he named his sons his story. *His story was in the names of his sons!* I have put away the past and now I can go toward the future unfettered. My life is fruitful in place of grief.

What does the apostle Paul say in the New Testament?

> *Brethren, I do not regard myself as having laid hold of it yet; but one thing I do:* forgetting what lies behind *and* reaching forward *to what lies ahead,* I press on *toward the goal for the prize of the upward call of God in Christ Jesus. (Phil. 3:13–14)*

That's a wow verse! *Forgetting the past, (Manasseh) I press on toward the future (Ephraim).* It's the upward call of God in Christ Jesus! That's what Joseph did. He let the past be in the past so that he could enjoy the future. When we don't let go of hurts in our past, a black cloud lingers. Putting away the past lifts the cloud so the sun shines through. Holding on to hurts complicates the present in such a way as to put a damper on the future. Holding on to our past hinders future momentum. We get stuck! We are fearful. We can't make friends that last. We see life in a negative bent. We think people are out to get us. We cannot move forward. Things said to us we take personally and get hurt quickly all over again.

What Are You Holding On To?

My question to the reader: Is there something or someone in your past who has hurt you beyond repair? You have wrestled and wrestled but the pain is still there. You can't believe someone has been so insensitive. You wallow in it, you dream about it, you have conversations with yourself over it. It doesn't seem to go away. It is hurt piled upon hurt. Is it a family member you can't forgive? Is it a friend who has hurt you more times than you can count? Is it a boss at work or one in authority? Is it a church member or a pastor?

I will say to you that you need a Manasseh. You need to once and for all put your stake in the ground and tell the Lord you are done with the hurt and the pain and the aggravation of the past. You have built mountains out of the pain. It's too high. You can't do this anymore. You can't continue to live like this. You are done! Cry out to Him in your agony. Let it go! The cancer of bitterness is permeating your very soul. Oh, you have good days when you don't think about the pain. But when you are not looking, or least thinking about the pain, there it is again, stabbing and debilitating.

Only as you have a Manasseh can you ever have an Ephraim. You need to be free to move forward, to go where God wants you to go, to do what God wants you to do. You must forgive those who have hurt you and put it away from your thoughts and dreams and aspirations. The hurts of your past are holding you down.

We all want an Ephraim, we want the future to be bright, but you can't have an Ephraim without first a Manasseh. Do you see that?

Different Kinds of Pain

Momentary Pain

There are different kinds of pain. There is the momentary hurt from a loved one that you know doesn't mean much. You can get over it quickly because you understand the person meant no harm. Those pains are minor in day-to-day living. They don't last long so you forget them easily. These kinds of hurts don't affect your life much.

Deep Pain

Then there is the kind of pain that is severe and long-lasting. You may have suffered abuse in childhood by a trusted relative, parent, or friend. It may be physical, sexual, or emotional abuse where you were simply the victim. Pain was inflicted upon you at a very vulnerable age. The memories are painful. And if you have to sometimes see that person, it's even more traumatic. The pain is deep.

The pain of losing a child, no matter the age, is severe and never seems to end. It may have been something you did to yourself, like an abortion. You have blamed yourself or others for going ahead with the abortion. It may be a miscarriage in the early months of pregnancy. It may be a disease or disability that your child had and didn't survive the trauma. It may have also come from outside your home, like a murder or an accident. Whenever it is the loss of a child, deep and lasting sorrow can overcome you at moments when you least expect it.

There is also pain that is suffered from what you thought was a solid friendship. You've been betrayed. Jesus spent three years with

Judas, and He knew Judas would betray him. How that must have hurt. David also was betrayed by his own father-in-law, Saul, who had befriended him and had given his daughter to David in marriage. David's pain was very deep. Saul was family. Saul was also the father of his very best friend and brother-in-law, Jonathan. This kind of pain may take years to wrestle through. It may take getting perspective through wise counsel. But more than that it takes a willing heart to see from God's viewpoint why the hurt was in your life in the first place. What can you learn from it? Will you bow the knee to God? Will you give it up?

Sometimes people hurt us because they too have been wounded, in different ways and different times, and we may not understand their woundedness. I covered this in the chapter where the brothers who are wounded by their dad turn the tables and wound their younger brother. We don't always understand where a person is coming from when they are angry and lash out. It may not have anything to do with us at the time, but a culmination of wounds they are trying to deal with. We certainly don't know all the answers. God does. He sees all our hearts at once and knows why we do what we do, when we don't even understand ourselves. Forgiving is always a God-thing. It never flows out of our own hearts. It always flows from the Father's heart to the Son's heart, to the Holy Spirit's heart right into ours.

You may say, I was abused as a child. I cannot forgive. It was too horrible. Or the person I thought was my friend hurt me beyond my ability to forgive. No, it's too deep. Or my character has been maligned. I was given a raw deal at work. The other person just went on with life as if nothing happened. My life was ruined. You may have gone through a very bitter divorce and lost everything. You may have been betrayed by your spouse, your parent, your child, your best friend, or your boss.

We must understand that wounded people wound people. Sometimes their own pain is so great that they unknowingly inflict pain on others. They may not understand the wounding that takes place. It also stands to reason that when we are wounded and our pain is great that it's difficult to see the sin in our own hearts. We may be angry or bitter and say things we shouldn't, which can and does make matters worse.

If God Was God, Could He Not Have Prevented the Pain?

It is a malady of human nature that when something goes wrong we first blame the person who caused the pain, whether that be self or someone else. Then, like Adam before us, we first of all blame the person we think is at fault, but ultimately we turn the blame to God. There are some hurts that we feel God could have stopped if He had wanted to. But He didn't. We think God chose to hurt us and cause us pain. So not only do we have a hurt inflicted by a person, we now believe God didn't do anything to help the situation. We blame God. We accuse Him. He didn't come through for us. He told us He loved us. Well, what kind of love is that? What kind of a God would allow pain and suffering to continue?

If we fail to deal with all kinds of hurts that come into our lives, they will just pile up like a mountain till we can't even see what started it all. It then spreads like a cancer into anger, resentment, bitterness, suspicion, distrust, and finally hatred toward another person. Hurt and pain, piled upon each other, affect *all* our relationships.

Back in chapter 7 I told you, the reader, of our woundedness in the workplace. It was a deep painful gash in our lives. Don and I handled it quite differently as men and women generally do. Let me explain now how the story of Joseph took place in my own life. When we were wounded, I cried on and off for about five years. I went through the what-ifs and if-onlys a thousand times in my mind. I couldn't believe godly people could wound so deeply and seemingly not care. How can people just go on with life as if nothing happened? I also wrestled with the Lord time and time again on how *He* could have let that wound happen without doing anything about it. As I read and then taught on Joseph, what stood out to me was his statement when naming Manasseh. "I have forgotten the pain of my father's household." I realized then that he hadn't forgotten. He forgave, and therefore, he was done with it. The pain became less and less as time wore on. He put his unforgiving spirit away. When at times he picked his woundedness back up, God reminded him (Manasseh) that he had already let it go.

That's what happened to me. I put it away. I put the wound at the feet of Him who had been deeply wounded Himself. When I picked it up again, and I did, He reminded me that it was now His wound and He would bear it, not me. I gave it up to Him again and again, and the more I did that, *the less pain I experienced.* The other thing I did was pray for "my enemies." They really weren't my enemies, but that was the category in which I had placed them. The more I prayed for success in their lives, *the less the pain bothered me.* I had my Manasseh in the prison of my mind. It was then that I could go on and have my Ephraim. My future was in His hands as it had always been, and I started to see that God was using me in the place where He wanted me. I then began to actively thank God for those people who had wounded us. As I prayed for blessing for them instead of wanting them to fail, *the sting of pain amazingly began to subside. The more I wanted God to bless them, the happier I became.*

Today those relationships that were raw with wounds have now become whole again. I held no animosity, no bitterness. And, lo and behold, there was no pain! The relationships have been restored, and Don and I have been honored in that place of woundedness. Only God can do this. Only He can take bitterness and pain and hurt and disappointment and nail it to His cross to be borne by Him so that we don't have to bear it anymore. Those very people where the wounds came from are friends. We email, we write, we talk, and we rejoice in all that God has done with them and with us. We are *all* blessed in the place where God has us.

I hope this helps you in your areas of wounding. It took five years for me to get to the point that God could turn the tables around for good. It took till ten years to be restored. The honoring came in the thirtieth year—a long time, to be sure. But God knows the timing, and He also knows how He has to mature us to be all He knows we can be.

> *Time, plus praying for blessing, plus thanksgiving, equals healing. There is no shortcut.*

I was on that prison floor with Joseph when he gave it all up. I was also with him in the honoring of his life when God elevated him. The next chapter in his life could have never taken place had not the holy ground of prison wrested his wounds from him and placed them squarely on a God who can and does take it. He died for our sins so that we might be healed.

> He *Himself* bore our sins *in His body* on the cross, *so that we might die to sin and live to righteousness; for by His wounds you were healed.* (1 Pet. 2:24)

Have there been other times of wounding since then? You bet! But the lessons I learned from Joseph have carried me through other times and other wounds. I am quicker to see God's hand than ever before. I am more easily swayed by "spiritual answers" without rebelling and wanting to take revenge. In watching my own grown children being wounded I know more fully how to pray for them. God is working in their lives, the same as He works in mine and in Joseph's and others whom He uses for the building of His Kingdom. My own children are not exempt from the wounds of life, neither will my grandchildren be. We who want to follow Jesus Christ will walk through the pain of wounding throughout our lives. Will we submit? Will God get the glory? Will our children and grandchildren learn the same lessons? The answer is a resounding *yes!*

Why Revenge Doesn't Work?

Sometimes we feel the only way to get even with a person is to retaliate, to hurt them back, to inflict pain so they will understand what we went through. Does that really work? Does that person really feel the same pain? No. But somehow we are duped into believing that if we retaliate, the situation will right itself.

But the problem is that God hasn't turned that authority over to us to inflict pain on someone else.

> *Never take your own revenge, beloved, but leave room for the wrath of God, for it is written, "Vengeance is Mine, I will repay," says the Lord. (Rom. 12:19)*

> *For we know Him who said, "Vengeance is Mine, I will repay." And again, "The Lord will judge His people." (Heb. 10:30)*

Why does God want us to leave the revenge to Him? Because He knows that there is sin in every human heart. God doesn't have sin to deal with. So when He takes revenge, he does it out of love and mercy. When I take revenge, I do it out of anger or resentment. It usually backfires for me. God is the only one who draws people to Himself when He takes revenge because He does it out a heart of mercy. We have a skewed sinful nature.

> *The heart is more deceitful than all else and is desperately sick, who can understand it? (Jer. 17:9)*

Really? Will God actually take revenge? Well, when? We want Him to act *now*! He will do the wooing and winning in His time, not ours. He knows just what to do and when to do it with every single person on planet earth. It's difficult to leave this up to Him but we must.

Forgiveness: An Expensive Option

Dr. Ralph Woerner, in his powerful tract on "Overcoming Hurt" (1992), has made some amazing statements. Thoughts in this next section will be excerpted from his paper.

The only option open to us to relieve pain is to forgive the other person. It's a very costly decision. Why? Because the cost is always borne by the one doing the forgiving. Forgiveness writes off the offense, whether or not you feel like it. Its' an act of the will. You choose to forgive, whether the other party has asked for it or not. If you need to forgive yourself, you choose that as well. Forgiveness is always a choice we have. We can harbor unforgiveness in our heart, or we can *choose* to forgive.

Forgiveness is always a "God thing." We are not capable of forgiving without the power of the Holy Spirit. Jesus showed the way of forgiveness when He forgave us. He modeled it. He knows that when we forgive we are released from bondage.

> *For if you forgive others for their transgressions, your heavenly Father will also forgive you. But if*

*you do not forgive others, then your Father will not
forgive your transgressions. (Matt. 6:14–15)*

Wow, forgiveness is in direct proportion to all that we have been forgiven at the cross. When we forgive, we are letting our offender off the hook. We are releasing him from the obligation to repay what he owes, from the need to apologize for what he has done, from the need to make a wrong right.

Forgiveness is an act of the will. *It is a clear and deliberate choice.* This doesn't mean we feel any better about what happened, nor does it mean the damage wasn't real. *Forgiveness doesn't excuse the behavior of the one wounding.* There may be consequences, either personal or legal, that need to take place. Forgiveness doesn't cover over the wrong, as if it never happened.

Forgiveness means we've chosen to release our offender from what he owes. Once this is done, the healing process is free to begin. Sometimes forgiveness brings instant release. At other times it may take months or years for our emotions to catch up with the action our will has taken. We will need to remind ourselves, "I have forgiven. I am done. I don't feel it yet, but it is done."

The person may need to be confronted on the hurt inflicted. Remember, the one inflicting pain doesn't feel the pain of the wounded. It would be like me stabbing you. You bleed and feel the pain. I may watch, but I do not feel the pain. That's the problem with each of us who wound another. We do not feel the pain of another. We can, however, understand that what we said or did caused pain.

Physical and emotional health is tied to our willingness to forgive. You can forgive the offender, or you can nurse a grudge. The reason we don't want to forgive is we don't want to give up our right to collect on what is owed, an apology. Some people refuse to forgive because they would rather talk about the problem and use it as a crutch to get sympathy from others.

Forgiveness doesn't mean we'll be unable to remember what happened. It doesn't cause our memory to fail. We don't get amnesia. Forgetting the incident means we've gotten over the *pain* that it caused. We no longer want our offender to suffer for what he's done. We no longer feel resentment toward him or wish him ill. This doesn't mean that we'll want to reestablish a close relationship with that person. Trust may need to be earned. The deeper the hurt, the longer it may take to heal. Our emotions don't always keep pace with our wills, but one morning we will awaken and not feel the pain of the situation or the need for revenge. Some situations will require confrontation before reconciliation is possible. You will know in your heart which ones need this step.

God expects of us, His children, to be able to forgive hurts and wrongs done to us. He will forgive as we forgive. This was the purpose for the cross. We could have never repaid Him for all the wrongs done. We could never apologize enough. So He went to the cross and died for every petty sin and every huge sin we are capable of committing. When He forgave at the cross, and we accepted His forgiveness, He then expects us to forgive those who have wronged us. It does set us free.

The timing of forgiveness is an important issue. Sometimes we are able to forgive right away. At other times the pain is so deep we will need time to process the hurt, the conversations, and our hearts. But no wound is beyond the healing touch of the Father, the dying of the Son, and the conviction of the Spirit. The question is: are we going to go about the life of forgiveness or are we going to carry resentment to our grave?

When you forgive, you set the prisoner free. And strangely enough, the prisoner you end up freeing most is yourself. So true in every life who has been wounded. We want to be free. God wants us to be free. There are steps to take. Will we do what is necessary to set ourselves free from the bleeding wounds that threaten to overtake our minds?

As we take a lesson from the life of Joseph (he is in the cloud of witnesses of Hebrew 12:1), he speaks to us of putting the past away and forgiving those who hurt us. In that respect he is a "type" of Christ in the Old Testament, showing us the way. Christ forgave as He suffered and bled and died, so that as we accept His forgiveness, He brings new life and our future is bright, no matter our circumstances. Take the cup of cold water Joseph offers as we run our race. That cup refreshes and gives us strength to finish our race in life.

What about Emotions?

Emotions are tricky. Making a decision to give up the past doesn't always flood us with peace and serenity. Decisions to put the past away may be made one day and much later emotions follow. How long that takes for the emotions to catch up to the act of laying wounds at the feet of Jesus, only God knows. Peace will come. Memories will give up the pain eventually. Don't be concerned how long it takes. Depending on the depth of the hurt, it may take between two to ten years. It depends on how deep the pain of the wound. Some wounds take more time to heal, others much less time.

Part of being wounded is the mourning that accompanies it. When we lose anything— whether it be a marriage, a child, a job, a title, a position, someone in the family—we are entering the process of mourning. We will go through the stages from "I can't believe this happened" to anger, to depression, and back and forth numerous times between those emotions. It's okay. This too takes time and prayer and sometimes counseling to get through. You will know. Forgiveness is an act of the will. Do we feel like forgiving? Probably not. You choose forgiveness, whether or not the other person has asked for it. Letting go of the past takes time. Sometimes a very long time. We can't rush these issues of the heart.

We don't have all the pieces to this puzzle called life. God does. Remember, "*All* things work together for good, to those who love

Him and are called *according to His purpose.*" (Rom. 8:28) Wow! Is there a better statement than that? Whatever you and I are going through right now is for His Purpose. Whatever pain, whatever joy, whatever heartache, it's to make us more like His Dear Son. At the cross we have been forgiven much. Can we not also forgive those who have wronged and hurt us?

Questions for Chapter 10

1) Explain the meaning of Manasseh. How has this meaning ministered to you in what you are going through?

2) Why is it important to have a Manasseh before an Ephraim?

3) Have you tried to have an Ephraim but are still wrestling with a Manasseh?

4) Why is praying for blessing and forgiveness so important?

5) What steps do you need to take in your life right now to let go of hurts?

CHAPTER 11

CRISIS MANAGEMENT

When Joseph became vice-chancellor, the next seven years were amazing, both personally and for the nation. Just enough sunshine, just enough rain. The crops were bountiful. There was food to sell. There was food to give away. There was nothing for which you couldn't buy or trade in those seven years. Everyone was happy and dancing and singing. Life was good. It would always be this way. Maybe it was God. Maybe it was a whole bunch of gods. Maybe it was human ingenuity. However you looked at it, life was good. Egypt was a model of prosperity. The surrounding nations were experiencing the same.

We have the mistaken idea that good times are here to stay. The problem is, those times don't last. When times are good, life is good. We rarely ever expect times to get worse, only better. It's in our DNA.

Joseph's personal life had taken on meaning. He had a position of authority he could never have dreamed possible. He had a wife and two adorable sons. Life was indeed good. And God was good. But Joseph, above all people, knew this wouldn't last. He and Pharaoh had planned and prepared for the economic downturn. They didn't know the day or the month, but they knew and so were not surprised when out of nowhere it hit! It stopped raining. The drought began.

The crops were in shambles. Grasshoppers multiplied and ate everything in sight. The hurricanes were so bad even the astrologers were astounded.

The first couple years into the downturn people relied on the granaries, which had been filled to capacity. They had saved enough for a "rainy day." But their savings were dwindling. The water stores were drying up. The market tables were bare. The carts stopped bringing produce. Day by day women were worried that there wasn't going to be enough food to feed growing children. Bellies had already begun to swell.

Fathers were worried that the measly crops they could grow wouldn't be enough to store away for months when nothing would grow. Money was running low. For some, there was no money at all. There weren't government subsidies to distribute. The existing governments were hoarding for the people at the top, who had money and position. It was the people in the middle and bottom who suffered the most. Two years of the economic downturn passed. Money was scarce and so were crops to buy. Like most human beings the world over, no one had saved for a seven-year famine. It would be true of America today. Listen to the latest statistic for our own country, 2015.

Millions of Americans have no savings set aside for a rainy day, leaving them in serious jeopardy if financial calamity strikes. Roughly one-third of American adults don't have any emergency savings, meaning that over seventy-two million people have no cushion to fall back on if they lose a job or have to deal with another crisis, according to a survey released today by NeighborWorks America, a national nonprofit that supports communities. Among the 1,035 adults who took part in the poll, 34 percent had no money set aside for an emergency, while 47 percent said their savings would cover their living expenses for ninety days or less. ("Americans Have Little or No Money Saved," USA Today, 2015)

Because Pharaoh had listened to Joseph, in Egypt storage bins were full of grain. As he knew from the interpretations of his dreams there were still five more years to go before the fertility of the earth began to produce again. Did he believe in Joseph's God? We are not told but he sure must have had deep respect for Him as he watched Joseph worship and rely on his God. Because they were in authority there was plenty for them and their household.

Storing Up for a Rainy Day

Just because we don't know the past from the future doesn't mean we can't plan for the future. We plan, but God is the one who controls everything. Planning is a good thing, and I think the interpretations of Pharaoh's dreams are worth looking at for that reason.

God does want us to work hard to make a living. Work is established by God for our benefit. He designed the workweek in Genesis 1 before sin entered the world. He designed us with specific gifts to work different jobs that keep our world afloat. He gives wealth, and he gives poverty. Why both? He gives poverty so that we will learn how to take care of each other. He gives wealth so that we *will* take care of each other. We must learn how to give, but we must also learn how to receive. Both issues are important to our maturity.

There are many verses in scripture on money and why it can be a benefit or a curse, depending on how it is used. It says that the "love" of money is a bad thing, but money itself is neither good nor bad. It all depends how we view money. Does God give it, or do we get it without God? If we think that we have money because we are so intelligent, gifted, or cunning, then our thinking is faulty. But if we always see money or wealth given as a gift from God, which can be taken away at any time, then we are thinking wisely. We will be grateful for what we have and will help others. When we are in need, we learn to pray specifically and watch as God meets our needs through others.

We are encouraged to store up for a rainy day. Investing is a good thing. Saving is a good thing. Tithing is a good thing. Taking care of our families is a good thing. Someone once said, "Live as though Christ is coming today, but prepare as though His return is a long way off." There is truth in that saying. Each day should be lived for Him who controls everything. Each plan is to take care of family and lineage after us. But each day should be one dedicated to the God of the universe who knows the past from the future.

Often God gives us warning of impending disaster. In our day and age the stock market is one indicator of good times or hard times. The stock market happens to go up or down in regard to cycles. If you are a believer in the Bible and God's warnings, they happen like clockwork roughly every seven years. If you are an economist, it happens every seven years. You can take your pick. Believe in the cycles of the Bible or believe your stock market analysts. Either way, seven years is a good number to go by. It was so with Joseph and Pharaoh's dreams of seven years/seven years.

I will choose to go by biblical data and warnings that God gives people in order to turn their hearts to Him. He knows that we need a jolt sometimes so we won't continue to go our own way, thinking we are smart and thinking that it's our own brains that make us prosper. Downturns have a way of humbling us and causing us to turn our hearts toward God. The good times don't cause us to do this, but the bad times do. When things are going well for us, we rarely pray about our finances. However, when we run out of money before the end of the month, we tend to pray a lot more. We know somehow that it is God who sustains us. We are not as aware of that when we don't have a need.

I have been faithful in keeping a journal for many years. When we were in our thirties, with four young children under our belts, we found ourselves without an income for a period of almost four years. It was during that time we taught our children to pray very specifically for our every need. Our children learned to pray. They learned to trust the Lord for finances and our faith grew immeasurably. God met every need we had, not all our wants, but every single need we had week after week, month after month, and year after year. We were never past due on a bill. It was a very special time in our young family as we learned to be very specific in our prayer requests. We watched as God met the needs very specifically down to the dollar! I still pray specifically instead of generally. I see many more answers to prayer that way. And I have learned to trust God in ways I could never have imagined. Does He bring poverty? Yes. Does He also bring abundance? A resounding yes. Both are for the purpose of trust in a Sovereign God.

Is God in Control?

When Pharaoh had his two dreams they were prophetical in nature. He didn't understand the implications until they were explained by a man of faith. I once heard it said that "prophecy is given, not to scare us but to prepare us." In essence that's the picture we have here. The prophecy was given so that those in leadership would be wise in the first seven years when everything looked as if it couldn't get better. For most people the world over, that's what we do when prosperity appears to be unending. We don't prepare for what can happen when the bottom falls out. This prophecy and every other prophecy in the Bible needs to be heeded. It will usually take a person of faith to explain to others what will happen in the future. Prophecies are given so that we will prepare for what is ahead. In that preparation, knowledge is given so we can help others in time of need. Joseph and Pharaoh didn't put away in granaries so they could hoard it for themselves. They put away so they could be generous and give to those in need.

What was important about the seven years of plenty? What was important about the beginning of the famine? It was to show Joseph, and all who would listen, that God is a God of His Word. He speaks; you listen. He predicts, and it happens. Is He real? Is He knowable? Does He know what He is doing in history? Did He orchestrate every single aspect of Joseph's life? Joseph is beginning to "get it." Joseph had a deep understanding of who God was and that He was sovereign over the events of individual men and nations alike. He brings rain. He withholds rain. He brings abundance. He withholds abundance. He gives wealth. He also gives poverty. Why? To show all human beings who it is that controls destinies. To show us that He has the whole world in His hands. He knows what He is doing, and He knows why. Listen to these verses:

> *He made from one man every nation of mankind to live on all the face of the earth, having determined their appointed times and the boundaries of their habitation, that they would seek God, if perhaps they might grope for Him and find Him, though He is not far from each one of us; for in Him we live and move and exist.*
> *(Acts 17:26–28)*

> *The Lord has established His throne in the heavens, and His sovereignty rules over all. (Ps. 103:19)*

> *The Lord makes poor and rich;*
> *He brings low, He also exalts.*
> *(1 Sam. 2:7)*

Nothing in Scripture is there by accident. Joseph was not in Egypt by accident. He hadn't been put in prison by accident. The cupbearer was not in prison by accident. Pharaoh's dreams were not by accident. All events happened by the Almighty hand of a sovereign God who is ruler over all things and all nations. He puts people in power. He takes people out of power. *He is sovereign.* He is in control, whether or not it appears that way!

How about our nation of America? Have our blessings come by accident? How about presidents, Congress, and the Supreme Court? Are they in power by accident? As we encounter the story of events of Joseph's time we must also ask ourselves the same questions. Is God sovereign? Does He control the events of history? And if so, why and for what purpose are events controlled? How long does He allow disobedience before He steps in? Are we puppets on a string or does God allow leverage in order that we might wake up to His plans for people and nations? Do we really believe that God is the blessed controller of all things? Do we really believe that God is in control of America? And our individual lives? Does this verse apply to us as well as for the people of Joseph's day?

> *For the Lord your God is bringing you into a good land, a land of brooks of water, of fountains and springs, flowing forth in valleys and hills. (Deut. 8:7)*

Did Joseph just happen to name his sons what he did? No, he named his sons "his story with God" because God actually named them while in the womb.

> *And pay attention, you peoples from afar. The Lord called Me from the womb; From the body of My mother He named Me. (Isa. 49:1)*

If that's the case, God put into Joseph's heart the names of Manasseh and Ephraim. These two names had meaning. God would not only use those names in Joseph's life, but He has used those names in my life as well. I understand God's control as I see it fully enacted in someone else's life. As I study the life of Joseph, I too say, "If he can have that attitude, I can too!" It's sometimes easier to see God's hand in someone else's life, but more tricky when it comes to our own life.

As we wrestle with past hurts and God's sovereignty, we will come to one of two conclusions:

God is not *in control, I am.* Therefore I will not forgive those who hurt me. They don't deserve my forgiveness. Therefore, I will not give it. The hurt was deep, insensitive, and so monstrous that I will never forgive them. I will control my future as I have done my past. No one will ever hurt me that deeply again!

Or *God is in control, and He knows what He is doing.* Therefore, I can and will forgive those who hurt me. God has a higher purpose for the hurt that I cannot see right now. He is asking me to trust Him. He is asking me to put the past behind me so I can move forward.

Which one have you chosen to enact? Are you living with hurt and pain that you will never let go of? Are you digging your heels in and saying no? It has affected you for years and you are not about to give it up, or have you put it away from your heart and at the feet of Jesus?

Forgiveness Affects Not Only My Past but My Future

I forgive not because the other person needs my forgiveness or has even asked for it, I forgive because *I* need to forgive! I need to be free of the hurt from others. There is *nothing* beyond the reach of forgiveness by God; therefore, it's not out of my reach to forgive. If God can forgive my sins, then I am able to forgive those who have hurt me (big hurts or small). I am made in His image; therefore, whatever He can do, He can do it through me. Forgiveness drove Him to the cross. Forgiveness should drive me to Him.

Joseph was flat on his face before the Lord when he forgave his brothers. Notice he forgave them, never knowing if he would ever see them again. He forgave them *before* they came to Egypt. He forgave because that's what God required of him, never knowing if they would ask for forgiveness or not. This wrestling match in prison affected the rest of his life. We are going to see the result of it in his future. Those two years were the most difficult but the most blessed of his life. We will witness his changed perspective to his brothers shortly.

The Famine Affects Surrounding Nations

Eventually the famine was so severe it was affecting the tribes of Israel (Jacob), the people known as Hebrews. It was touching the lineage of the coming Messiah. Word came to village after village that Egypt had grain.

"Really? Did they really? I wonder if they would sell some to families who are suffering?" This was the question on the minds of the grown men of the tribes of Israel (Jacob). They wondered if a few of the brothers went to Egypt would they be able to come home with grain enough to feed their children. They talked it over with their elderly father, Jacob, and came up with a plan. Maybe if they all went there would be enough grain to feed all their families. The only stipulation that Jacob had was that Benjamin could not go. If none of them came back, he would still have one son. They understood Jacob's reluctance to let Joseph's brother go with them. They didn't want to hurt their father again as deeply as they had hurt him twenty years ago.

Isn't it interesting that not one of the brothers in that twenty-year span ever spilled the beans to Jacob about what they had done to Joseph? They harbored the secret within their brother unit. Amazing. Of course they had no idea if Joseph was still alive. He was alive when they last saw him but assumed that probably as a slave Joseph wouldn't still be alive. Slaves often didn't live long lives. They were malnourished and overworked. That scenario more than likely was talked about when they were alone with each other. Did they wonder? Yes, from time to time they probably did. If they talked among themselves, it would have never been in earshot of their dad. Most of the time they just didn't talk about it, afraid that even in talking Jacob might hear.

As men often do, they put it behind them (compartmentalize it) and went on with their lives, raising families and earning a living. Men's brains function compartmentally. Work was in a box, family was in its own box, secrets were in a separate box. They compartmentalized everything they did.

Jacob had raised his sons to be hard workers and they were. Each was responsible for his own family. Cousins played together. Cousins worked together. Theirs was a close-knit clan. Jacob was still the patriarch of the family and would be until his death. And then each of them would become the patriarchs of their own family clan. They were still small in number. The ten brothers families had grown to around seventy. Multiplication was taking place even though their clan was the smallest in the area of Canaanite clans.

God needed a Hebrew with Egyptian authority for such a time as this, a fellow Hebrew who could do something for his relatives, a fellow Hebrew who understood family, who understood loyalty, who understood hurt, who understood forgiveness. That Joseph became that man was by the mighty hand of an Almighty God who orchestrates men and women to be molded into His image for His purposes. God had a plan, and it could not be thwarted, undone, altered, or manipulated.

Are you being molded for the purposes of God? Are you putty in His hand? You may not understand His ways. You may not understand the times in which you live. You may not understand much. But understanding isn't important. What is important is, have you bowed the knee? Have you given him your whole life to be used as He sees fit? Have you become pliable so that He can use you in any given circumstance? In your neighborhood, in your church, in your place of business, in any country, in any nation to which He sends you?

You could look at Joseph at this point and say that he was a godly man with a godly perspective; therefore, God was going to use him. No, Joseph had gone the route of trying to control his destiny. It hadn't worked. All he knew was that God was in control and he wasn't. He didn't know much more than that. He understood Pharaoh's dreams and put an economic plan together to survive the coming collapse of Egypt and the surrounding nations. He had no clue what God was going to do next. His was obedience on a molecular level. It was a daily following Him who knew the future. That's all he knew for sure.

He wasn't godly; therefore, God would use him. No, it's the other way around. God used him, causing him to see God's perspective. Therefore, he became godly in his attitude and thoughts. He didn't know the future, God did. He had passed some significant tests, so God knew He would be usable for His glory. But this time, as in times past, Joseph didn't see coming what was just around the corner. Will he be tested again?

Don't get me wrong, I am sure Joseph was grateful he was out of prison. He was grateful for the amazing position he found himself in. But I know that Joseph knew he wasn't there because he was so clever or knew how to interpret dreams or was so smart. He was in that position because God had placed him there. Of that he knew. More than that he probably didn't know. How could he have known what was coming next? He wasn't God. He had no visions of grandeur. He was taking each day as it came, knowing God would show him the way. He knew a famine was coming, but that's all he knew.

Questions for Chapter 11

1) How often have you tried to control your circumstances? When you do, what happens?

2) Explain sovereignty. In what ways has that helped you understand God's plan for your life?

3) Give your evaluation of America at this point in time. Have we been here before? Or are things different now?

CHAPTER 12

TEST NUMBER FOUR

He sent a man before them,
Joseph, who was sold as a slave.
They afflicted his feet with fetters,
He himself was laid in irons;
Until the time that his word came to pass,
The word of the Lord tested him.
The king sent and released him,
The ruler of peoples, and set him free.
He made him lord of his house
And ruler over all his possessions,
To imprison his princes at will,
That he might teach his elders wisdom.
Israel also came into Egypt;
Thus Jacob sojourned in the land of Ham.
And He caused His people to be very fruitful,
And made them stronger than their adversaries.
(Ps. 105:17–24)

The Wounded Come Calling

Joseph was fulfilled day after day. He loved his job. He knew God had given him gifts he needed to understand the times and to understand numbers and economies. He could now praise God for all that had taken place in his life. He had put the past behind him. Being given a job he hadn't asked for but was cut out to do was a pleasure. Joseph had leadership abilities that he loved using for the glory of God. Life was good, and God was good. Those two things he cherished and lived for.

Now we come to the part of the story that you know best. The following is the sermon you have heard from pastors, Sunday school teachers, and theologians the world over. One day, as Joseph was going about his business of overseeing the giving of grain to foreigners, there came a group of men.

Let's first listen in on the brothers' conversation with their father, Jacob, before coming to Egypt.

> Now Jacob saw that there was grain in Egypt, and Jacob said to his sons, "Why are you staring at one another?" He said, "Behold, I have heard that there is grain in Egypt; go down there and buy some for us from that place, so that we may live and not die." Then ten brothers of Joseph went down to buy grain from Egypt. But Jacob did not send Joseph's brother Benjamin with his brothers, for he said, "I am afraid that harm may befall him." So the sons of Israel came to buy grain among those who were coming, for the famine was in the land of Canaan also. (Gen. 42:1-5)

Surprise: Another Test

Now Joseph was the ruler over the land; he was the one who sold to all the people of the land. And Joseph's brothers came and bowed down to him with their faces to the ground. *When Joseph saw his brothers he recognized them, but he disguised himself to them and spoke to them harshly. And he said to them, "Where have you come from?" And they said, "From the land of Canaan, to buy food. "But Joseph had recognized his brothers, although they did not recognize him. Joseph* remembered the dreams *which he had about them. (Gen. 42:6–9)*

When Joseph saw his brothers he had to catch himself from emotion. *They bowed down!* The lights went on, and he almost gave himself away. Did they recognize him? No, they did not. After all, he wore royal Egyptian clothing and spoke Egyptian. His servants called him Master Zephenath. He spoke through an interpreter, so they didn't realize who he was.

He had to gather his thoughts quickly. Here were his ten brothers, standing before him, no, *bowing before him.* It was the same ten who had sold him. Oh, how he had wrestled with them in his thought life when he first came to Egypt. He had actually not thought much about them in the last nine years. He had been too busy storing grain for the coming famine. His workload had been heavy and constant. It had been so long since he had thought of the dreams, the dreams when he was young and foolish. And now here they were, bowing down to him! He was stunned. The dreams were real after all!

What should he do? For now he would just listen to what they are asking. Remember, all the conversations were through an interpreter.

> *"You are spies; you have come to look at the unde-fended parts of our land." Then they said to him, "No, my lord, but your servants have come to buy food. We are all sons of one man; we are honest men, your servants are not spies." Yet he said to them, "No, but you have come to look at the unde-fended parts of our land!" But they said, "Your servants are twelve brothers in all, the sons of one man in the land of Canaan; and behold, the youngest is with our father today,* and one is no longer alive." *Joseph said to them, "It is as I said to you, you are spies; by this you will be tested: by the life of Pharaoh, you shall not go from this place unless your youngest brother comes here! Send one of you that he may get your brother, while you remain confined, that your words may be tested, whether there is truth in you. But if not, by the life of Pharaoh, surely you are spies."* So he put them all together in prison for three days. *(Gen. 42:9–17)*

During the Three-Day Prison Sentence

It appears to me that Joseph made methodical and calculated decisions. He thought through something well before making the decision. We will talk about his spiritual gifts shortly. Joseph had to think how to respond to his brothers. By putting them in prison, was he doing to them what he thought about doing for those many years while he languished in prison? Did he have the fleeting thought,

"Serves them right! They can rot in prison for all I care!" If he did, then he realized once again who God was and why he was in Egypt. During that three-day period, he prayed. He wept. He asked God to show him what to do. I don't believe he slept. And God gave him a strategy. I also believe that when he went home in the evening to play with his two sons, each time he held Manasseh and kissed his cheeks, God reminded him of the meaning of that name Manasseh, "I have forgotten the pain of my father's household," "I have forgiven my brothers," "I have put it away."

O Lord, the God of my salvation,
I have cried out by day and in the night before
You.
(Ps. 88:1)

He had the power to leave them in prison. Would he take that way out? He had to listen to the still small voice of Almighty God who spoke in dreams, in visions, and in the middle of the night with sometimes whispers into his conscience. No, he would not "pay them back" for what they had done. He would listen, and he would do what God instructed him to do. God had given him Manasseh. He had forgiven the past betrayal. Would he now go back on that name, the child God had so clearly given to remind him?

In a dream, a vision of the night,
When sound sleep falls on men,
While they slumber in their beds.
(Job 33:15)

Did Joseph, as an adult now, recall his coat of many colors and how he had prided himself on what a great son he had been? He had elevated himself above them by telling them his dreams. Dreams he had all but forgotten. Did God give perspective to his mind that God was the One who had given him the two dreams and then sold him into slavery, not his brothers? God ripped him from his family and put him squarely in Egypt. God had elevated him to second position next to Pharaoh. God had a purpose in all that He allowed and how He had led. Those three days while his brothers were in prison, wondering if this was their fate forever, Joseph talked to God and God gave wisdom and perspective. I am very sure God brought up the names of Manasseh and Ephraim to his conscience.

God clearly gave him a strategy to release the brothers to go back home with their supply of food and money. He would keep one of them in Egypt in order to test their motives. Would they bring their youngest brother the next time they came? Who should he keep in prison? God gave that answer too.

> *Now Joseph said to them on the third day, "Do this and live, for I fear God: if you are honest men, let one of your brothers be confined in prison; but as for the rest of you, go, carry grain for the famine of your households, and bring your youngest brother to me, so your words may be verified, and you will not die." And they did so. Then they said to one another, "Truly we are guilty concerning our brother, because we saw the distress of his soul when he pleaded with us, yet we would not listen; therefore this distress has come upon us." Reuben answered them, saying, "Did I not tell you, 'Do not sin against the boy'; and you would not listen? Now comes the reckoning for his blood." They did not know, however, that Joseph understood, for there was an interpreter between them. He turned away from them and wept. But when he returned*

to them and spoke to them, he took Simeon from them and bound him before their eyes. (Gen. 42:18–24)

Isn't it interesting that twenty years had passed, and yet they all had total recall of that day so long ago when they sold their brother? They didn't know if he was dead or alive, but the memory was as fresh as if it had happened yesterday. We don't forget what happened to us, and we don't forget what we did to another to cause such pain and hurt.

When interviewing people who have suffered trauma, say in WWII, you watch as that man tells his story and out of nowhere, he starts crying. The memories trigger emotional responses in us we thought were long gone. I wonder if Joseph's brothers experienced the same emotion of that day so long ago when they decided to get rid of their little brother. Joseph asked the brothers to choose one among them to keep as a prisoner. They either did not, or could not.

Simeon Held Hostage

"He took Simeon from them and bound him before their eyes." Why Simeon? Did he enact the same binding they had done to him? This is only conjecture on my part, but earlier in the story when the brothers were conversing on what to do with "this dreamer," only Reuben and Judah were mentioned by name. Reuben didn't want to do any harm to Joseph. Judah suggested he be sold. Even though Scripture doesn't tell us, could it have been Simeon who came up with the plan to kill Joseph by putting him in a pit and leaving him? Judah said, "No, let's make a profit on him." Joseph chose Simeon. Was it random? Was he second to Reuben, so it followed logic? Or did Joseph know something from years long past? It's an interesting thought.

Then Joseph gave orders to fill their bags with grain and to restore every man's money in his sack, and to give them provisions for the journey. And thus it was done for them. So they loaded their donkeys with their grain and departed from there. As one of them opened his sack to give his donkey fodder at the lodging place, he saw his money; and behold, it was in the mouth of his sack. Then he said to his brothers, "My money has been returned, and behold, it is even in my sack." And their hearts sank, and they turned trembling to one another, saying, "What is this that God has done to us?" When they came to their father Jacob in the land of Canaan, they told him all that had happened to them, saying, "The man, the lord of the land, spoke harshly with us, and took us for spies of the country. But we said to him, 'We are honest men; we are not spies. We are twelve brothers, sons of our father; one is no longer alive, and the youngest is with our father today in the land of Canaan.' The man, the lord of the land, said to us, 'By this I will know that you are honest men: leave one of your brothers with me and take grain for the famine of your households, and go. But bring your youngest brother to me that I may know that you are not spies, but honest men. I will give your brother to you, and you may trade in the land.'" Now it came about as they were emptying their sacks, that behold, every man's bundle of money was in his sack; and when they and their father saw their bundles of money, they were dismayed. Their father Jacob said to them, "You have bereaved me

of my children: Joseph is no more, and Simeon is no more, and you would take Benjamin; all these things are against me." Then Reuben spoke to his father, saying, "You may put my two sons to death if I do not bring him back to you; put him in my care, and I will return him to you." But Jacob said, "My son shall not go down with you; for his brother is dead, and he alone is left. If harm should befall him on the journey you are taking, then you will bring my gray hair down to Sheol in sorrow." (Gen. 42:25–38)

We see that Jacob hadn't changed. He had been prejudiced toward Joseph and now it was Benjamin. I am sure the brothers still struggled with his prejudice but had gotten used to Jacob's ways. The ten sons have accepted his idiosyncrasies as normal. They are all in need of food, so right now empty stomachs are taking precedence over everything else. But Jacob will wait awhile, leaving Simeon in prison. Really? Really? I'm sure the brothers all talk about this when they go home to their own families. Jacob was an immovable object who thought highly of two sons to the detriment of the ten. Great family man, huh? It's a wonder that God chose Jacob—so sinful, so full of himself, so very prejudiced, still not telling the truth. Oh, so like us! I don't like Jacob because he reminds me of me. And you. And all of us. We certainly want to live the Christian life but find that in ourselves we are just Christians in sin skin. We talk like Christians, but more often than not, we don't act like Christians. Haven't changed much through the centuries, have we?

Let me break in here with God's choosing of the clans of Israel in order to bring about His Messiah. God chose not because of anything people did or were, he simply chooses because He chooses. Plain and simple. To Israel, God said:

The LORD did not set His love on you nor choose you because you were more in number than any of the peoples, for you were the fewest of all peoples. (Deut. 7:7)

Therefore say to the Israelites, 'This is what the Sovereign LORD says: It is not for your sake, people of Israel, that I am going to do these things, but for the sake of my holy name, which you have profaned among the nations where you have gone." (Ezek. 36:22)

Jacob, or Israel, and his sons were chosen because of God's sovereignty. Period. It was nothing they did. And we know it was not because they were all so righteous. Just the opposite. We see Jacob's callousness when he left his son Simeon in prison. He didn't want to lose Benjamin, now a grown man with ten sons of his own. Sometimes I wonder why God chose Jacob, but He did. Then I wonder why He chose me! But He did. We are all undeserving of His love, His care, and His leading. But aren't we glad He doesn't wait for us to deserve His love? That's called grace. It's also called mercy! We can see this over and over in Jacob's life. We are not told how long the brothers and their families survived on what Joseph gave them. It appears for quite a period of time.

The Famine Continues

Now the famine was severe in the land. So it came about when they had finished eating the grain which they had brought from Egypt, that their father said to them, "Go back, buy us a little food." Judah spoke to him, however, saying, "The man solemnly warned us, 'You shall not see my face unless your brother is with you.' If you send our brother with us, we will go down and buy you food. But if you do not send him, we will not go down; for the man said to us, 'You will not see my face unless your brother is with you.'" Then Israel said, "Why did you treat me so badly by telling the man whether you still had another brother?" But they said, "The man questioned particularly about us and our relatives, saying, 'Is your father still alive? Have you another brother?' So we answered his questions. Could we possibly know that he would say, 'Bring your brother down'?" (Gen. 43:1–7)

Jacob actually wanted his sons to lie. He had not changed his ways, nor his attitude. It was still all about Jacob. The more I read about this man, the more I see the reasoning behind why God took Joseph out of that dysfunctional family. A father who lied to get his way, and who overtly favored a couple sons over the others. Still a liar and a manipulator. Wow. Thank God Joseph was removed from all this.

It is a blessing from God when He removes us from our own dysfunctional families while we are young and teaches us to follow Him. All our families are dysfunctional in some ways if we are honest. He lets us stay for eighteen years, then we either learn to walk with Him or we walk like our family of origin. Your family of origin might have been great, if so you will copy the good things you saw and heard. If not, you will want to go a different path. It's a grace gift to us when God removes us and encourages us to stand on our own, but especially to learn from Him in spiritual ways. I know this was very true in my family. We went to church, but Christianity was not talked about in my home. We were taught moral values that were probably biblical in their origin, but never correlated to God and the Bible. Many homes are like that. Christianity is church on Sunday but during the week, it's never brought up.

One of the brothers will now step up to the plate and offer to be surety for Benjamin.

> Judah *said to his father Israel, "Send the lad with me and we will arise and go, that we may live and not die, we as well as you and our little ones. I myself will be surety for him; you may hold me responsible for him. If I do not bring him back to you and set him before you, then let me bear the blame before you forever. For if we had not delayed, surely by now we could have returned twice." (Gen. 43:8–10)*

How long this period of time was we don't know. Simeon was in prison for a time. I am sure Joseph checked on him, unknown to him. He wanted to make sure Simeon was treated well. But he also tested his brothers. Would they leave Simeon in prison and forget about him? Would his father, Jacob, leave Simeon in prison indefinitely as long as they had enough food? What would cause Jacob to send them back? Would they ever tell the truth about Joseph? Did any of the brothers ask why they weren't going back for Simeon? Were they concerned for his welfare? Or were they so submissive to Jacob as head of the clan that they didn't want to cross him?

> *Then their father Israel said to them, "If it must be so, then do this: take some of the best products of the land in your bags, and carry down to the man as a present, a little balm and a little honey, aromatic gum and myrrh, pistachio nuts and almonds. Take*

double the money in your hand, and take back in your hand the money that was returned in the mouth of your sacks; perhaps it was a mistake. Take your brother also, and arise, return to the man; and may God Almighty grant you compassion in the sight of the man, so that he will release to you your other brother and Benjamin. And as for me, if I am bereaved of my children, I am bereaved." So the men took this present, and they took double the money in their hand, and Benjamin; then they arose and went down to Egypt and stood before Joseph. (Gen. 43:11–15)

Finally Jacob gave up for the sake of their meager food supply. He finally saw that he couldn't save Benjamin any more than he could have saved Joseph. It was right to go back for food and to retrieve Simeon if possible. There were little ones to feed. He wouldn't let any more time to pass before meeting the growing need for sustenance in his growing family.

Questions for Chapter 12

1) Why is work beneficial for us?

2) Why does God bring famine or economic downturns?

3) Why is using our gifts important for us?

4) In your opinion, why would Joseph put all ten brothers in prison for three days?

5) Do you agree or disagree with me on why Joseph chose Simeon to be put in prison while the brothers went home.

6) Why do you think Judah becomes surety for Benjamin?

7) What was your family of origin like? Did you learn biblical truths? Were they caught as well as taught?

CHAPTER 13

SIBLING JOY

When Joseph saw Benjamin with them, he said to his house steward, "Bring the men into the house, and slay an animal and make ready; for the men are to dine with me at noon." So the man did as Joseph said, and brought the men to Joseph's house. Now the men were afraid, because they were brought to Joseph's house; and they said, "It is because of the money that was returned in our sacks the first time that we are being brought in, that he may seek occasion against us and fall upon us, and take us for slaves with our donkeys."

So they came near to Joseph's house steward, and spoke to him at the entrance of the house, and said, "Oh, my lord, we indeed came down the first time to buy food, and it came about when we came to the lodging place, that we opened our sacks, and behold, each man's money was in the mouth of his sack, our money in full. So we have brought it back in our hand. We have also brought down other money in our hand to buy food; we do not know who put our money in our sacks." He said, "Be at ease, do not be afraid. Your God (Elohim) and the God (Elohim) of your father has given you treasure in your sacks; I had your money." Then he brought Simeon out to them. Then the man brought the men into Joseph's house and gave them water, and they washed their feet; and he gave their donkeys fodder. So they prepared the present for Joseph's coming at noon; for they had heard that they were to eat a meal there. When Joseph came home, they brought into the house to him the present which was in their hand and bowed to the ground before him. (Gen. 43:16–26)

How Shall They Hear without a Preacher?

Verse 23 is very interesting to me. Did the servants of Joseph believe in his Hebrew God? What they said indicated that possibility. Joseph's servants knew all about his Elohim. Elohim means "maker of heaven and earth" and is the name pagans use when they become believers in the Hebrew God. This tells me Joseph shared his faith. Joseph would have had opportunities to talk to those who worked for him about His God. He was their overseer. They must have seen Joseph praying at times. They must have heard him express wisdom that only comes from Elohim. Yes, I believe his was faith worn openly, even though he was in a pagan culture. Because of his humility, he did not push his faith on anyone. He was patient, answering questions that came his way. How else could his servants have spoken of Elohim?

There is no scripture that tells us what he said in conversations to those around him or to his family. But one day we very likely will meet people whom Joseph led to a saving faith in the God of the

Hebrews. We do know he stood strong, sometimes all alone. But at other times, he professed his beliefs. Potiphar saw his abilities and put him in charge. The overseer of the prison put him in charge. Why? What did they see? Did they have conversations about Yahweh?

Who else would have been observant of Joseph's God? The cupbearer certainly would have had firsthand knowledge of Joseph's God. Pharaoh would have firsthand knowledge of the God of the Hebrews. After all, Joseph clearly told Pharaoh that it was his Elohim who had given the interpretation. Pharaoh would have wanted more information on this amazing God who understands times and seasons and accurately predicts the future. Yes, I am sure Pharaoh talked to Joseph about his faith. Did he become a brother in the faith? If he did, we will hear his amazing story in eternity future.

Joseph's wife certainly would have been another person asking and thinking and praying. She is not mentioned except at the marriage and birth of her sons. But her sons had Hebrew names with deep meaning. Was she a believer? We are not told, but I am going to assume that she knew Joseph's God and raised their sons accordingly.

When Joseph named Manasseh he was telling those around him that the past was forgiven and forgotten. Did people around him ask him why "Manasseh," and was he able to tell them his story? He would have had that opportunity with Pharaoh and those with whom he worked closely. Men in the workplace looked up to him. I believe this is why Pharaoh understood later on when Joseph wanted to bring his family to Egypt. Pharaoh amazingly gave him the best land in all of Egypt. He knew the story. He had walked alongside Joseph with the birth of his two sons. He knew. He honored his friend and companion.

With the birth of Ephraim, Joseph was indicating that blessings had come to him in the very land he occupied. That too would have spoken volumes to Pharaoh. Pharaoh was included in those fruitful blessings. Joseph melted into the Egyptian culture in language, dress, and customs; but he took his God with him into everything he did, into his marriage, into his leadership position. I imagine there were opportunities to talk about his Elohim in private conversation. Anyone with that strong of a faith talks about it when approached, lives it when in secret, prays openly in his home or at his desk. People around him watched. They always do. We do know that there will be people from every tribe and tongue in Heaven with us. This includes Egypt.

And they sang a new song, saying, "Worthy are You to take the book and to break its seals; for You were slain, and purchased for God with Your blood men from every tribe and tongue and people and nation. *(Rev. 5:9)*

How then will they call on Him in whom they have not believed? How will they believe in Him whom they have not heard? And how will they hear without a preacher? How will they preach unless they are sent? Just as it is written, "How beautiful are the feet of those who bring good news of good things!" However, they did not all heed the good news; for Isaiah says, "Lord, who has believed our report?" So faith comes from hearing, *and hearing by the word of Christ. But I say, surely they have never heard, have they? Indeed they have; "Their voice has gone out into all the earth, And their words to the ends of the world." But I say, surely Israel did not know, did they? First Moses says, "I will make you jealous by that which is not a nation, By a nation without understanding will I anger you." And Isaiah is very bold and says, "I*

was found by those who did not seek Me, I became
manifest to those who did not ask for Me." (Rom.
10:14–20)

The Reality of His Long-Forgotten Dreams

When his brothers came back and bowed to him once again, Joseph knew this time that his dream was to be fulfilled. The time when they were apart was an anxious time for Joseph. He badly wanted to see Benjamin, his only full brother. Since first seeing his brothers he had recounted the two dreams he had as a teen. Years ago he had been pained deeply and then angered about what they did. Then he had turned it all over to the God who heals wounds. He had put the past behind him and forgiven them, before he ever realized the dreams would be fulfilled.

He didn't have any idea he would ever see his brothers again. But now the dreams were real once again. He waited many months for them to return. Would they? Yes, he knew they would because now he understood that the dreams were a vision (prophetical in nature) God had given him long before they were to be fulfilled. How different from the dreams he had interpreted in prison for the cupbearer and then for Pharaoh. Those dreams had immediate fulfillment. His were only now coming to pass.

Now here they were again, bowing down to him. The emotion of it was more than he could hide. God had indeed been in the dreams. God had been in Egypt with him. God had been in prison with him. And now here were his brothers, coming to collect their other brother. They had not left Simeon to die. The change in them was obvious. Now he knew that God had been at work in their lives as He had been in his own.

Then he asked them about their welfare, and said,
"Is your old father well, of whom you spoke? Is he

still alive?" They said, "Your servant our father is well; he is still alive." They bowed down in homage. As he lifted his eyes and saw his brother Benjamin, his mother's son, he said, "Is this your youngest brother, of whom you spoke to me?" And he said, "May God be gracious to you, my son." Joseph hurried out for he was deeply stirred over his brother, and he sought a place to weep; and he entered his chamber and wept there. (Gen. 43:27–30)

Joseph could hardly contain his emotions when his brothers came back for Simeon. He had anticipated them bringing Benjamin. How awesome to see his little brother after twenty-two years. Benjamin had grown into a man who had a wife and ten sons. He had changed, but the love was still there for this little brother whom he helped raise as a baby and young child.

Then he washed his face and came out; and he controlled himself and said, "Serve the meal." So they served him by himself, and them by themselves, and the Egyptians who ate with him by themselves, (because the Egyptians could not eat bread with the Hebrews, for that is loathsome to the Egyptians.) (Gen. 43:31–32)

The Egyptian culture was very strict on laws and rules. One was that it was unlawful to eat with anyone not of your culture. The Egyptians undoubtedly were a wealthy culture and with wealth comes fame and a sense of entitlement and control. All foreigners ate by themselves or with their families. Eating with foreigners, even one who was your superior, was against the unstated rules of the culture. Joseph obeyed this mandate, as did his servants. Even though Joseph was in charge of everything he still could not eat at the same table with his own servants, or with Pharaoh.

Did his brothers pick up on this custom? Did they think it strange that everyone was in different sections of the room eating by themselves? And then they started looking around at the seating arrangement. Their astonishment didn't go unnoticed.

> *Now they were seated before him, the firstborn according to his birthright and the youngest according to his youth, and the men looked at one another in astonishment. He took portions to them from his own table, but Benjamin's portion was five times as much as any of theirs. So they feasted and drank freely with him. (Gen. 43:33-34)*

They watched in amazement. What was this? Joseph could give them food from *his* table? They knew the customs too, so were they talking about that at their table? Probably, as well as why was he taking so much interest in Benjamin? And Benjamin probably was saying, "No, I'm full. It's okay. I don't need any more food. I'm good." But the food kept coming his way.

Another Test for this Band of Brothers

> *Then he commanded his house steward, saying, "Fill the men's sacks with food, as much as they can carry, and put each man's money in the mouth of his sack. Put my cup, the silver cup, in the mouth of the sack of the youngest, and his money for the grain." And he did as Joseph had told him. As soon as it was light, the men were sent away, they with their donkeys. They had just gone out of*

the city, and were not far off, when Joseph said to his house steward, "Up, follow the men; and when you overtake them, say to them, 'Why have you repaid evil for good? Is not this the one from which my lord drinks and which he indeed uses for divination? You have done wrong in doing this.'" So he overtook them and spoke these words to them. They said to him, "Why does my lord speak such words as these? Far be it from your servants to do such a thing. Behold, the money which we found in the mouth of our sacks we have brought back to you from the land of Canaan. How then could we steal silver or gold from your lord's house? With whomever of your servants it is found, let him die, and we also will be my lord's slaves." So he said, "Now let it also be according to your words; he with whom it is found shall be my slave, and the rest of you shall be innocent." Then they hurried, each man lowered his sack to the ground, and each man opened his sack. He searched, beginning with the oldest and ending with the youngest, and the cup was found in Benjamin's sack. Then they tore their clothes, and when each man loaded his donkey, they returned to the city. When Judah and his brothers came to Joseph's house, he was still there, and they fell to the ground before him. Joseph said to them, "What is this deed that you have done? Do you not know that such a man as I can indeed practice divination?" So Judah said, "What can we say to my lord? What can we speak? And how can we justify ourselves? God has found out the iniquity of your servants; behold, we are my lord's slaves, both we and the one in whose possession the cup has been found." But he said, "Far be it from me to do this. The man in whose possession the cup has been found, he shall be my slave; but as for you, go up in peace to your father." (Gen. 44:1–17)

The Pleading of Judah

Then Judah approached him and said, "Oh my lord, may your servant please speak a word in my lord's ears, and do not be angry with your servant; for you are equal to Pharaoh. My lord asked his servants, saying, 'Have you a father or a brother?' We said to my lord, 'We have an old father and a little child of his old age. Now his brother is dead, so he alone is left of his mother, and his father loves him.' Then you said to your servants, 'Bring him down to me that I may set my eyes on him.' But we said to my lord, 'The lad cannot leave his father, for if he should leave his father, his father would die.' You said to your servants, however, 'Unless your youngest brother comes down with you, you will not see my face again.' Thus it came about when we went up to your servant my father, we told him the words of my lord. Our father said, 'Go back, buy us a little food.' But we said, 'We cannot go down. If our youngest brother is with us, then we will go down; for we cannot see the man's face unless our youngest brother is with us.' Your servant my father said to us, 'You know that my wife bore me two sons; and the one went out from me, and I said, "Surely he is torn in pieces," and

I have not seen him since. If you take this one also from me, and harm befalls him, you will bring my gray hair down to Sheol in sorrow.' Now, therefore, when I come to your servant my father, and the lad is not with us, since his life is bound up in the lad's life, when he sees that the lad is not with us, he will die. Thus your servants will bring the gray hair of your servant our father down to Sheol in sorrow. For your servant became surety for the lad to my father, saying, 'If I do not bring him back to you, then let me bear the blame before my father forever.' Now, therefore, please let your servant remain instead of the lad a slave to my lord, and let the lad go up with his brothers. For how shall I go up to my father if the lad is not with me—for fear that I see the evil that would overtake my father?" (Gen. 44:18–34)

It appears that Judah, being the one who sold Joseph, now became "surety" for Benjamin. He now negotiated not for selfish ends, but to redeem the brothers' misdeeds. It appears that Judah bears the responsibility among the brotherhood for the selling of Joseph and now for the safe return of Benjamin. Judah did indeed have a change of heart and would never do again what he had done to Joseph. Having relived his misdeeds over and over for the last twenty-two years, he was not about to behave in such a way as to send his father to an untimely death.

Remember too in the parentheses chapter (chapter 38) that Judah had been dealing with his own trauma in family affairs. He had learned and matured. God indeed had been with him, brought him through his own trials so that Judah was looking to the Lord for life. Judah too had had sorrow of his own, had played the what-ifs and if-onlys as well and had come to the conclusion that God was a sovereign God who controls destinies and directs lives. He now had twin sons from Tamar to prove that God can and will do as He chooses. God's ways truly are not our ways. He sees the big picture, we only see the parts.

The tests that Joseph laid upon his brothers demonstrated that he knew who in the group betrayed him. He wanted to see if change had taken place in them. Joseph saw that Judah would never do to another brother as he had done to Joseph. Judah was willing to give his own life for the life of his youngest brother. He also showed great compassion for his elderly father, as he didn't want anything he would do to cause him any more sorrow or cause his death.

Had Judah grieved at watching his father for the past two decades and felt he could do nothing about it? Did he ever want to tell Jacob what he had done? Being a close-knit family, the brothers knew of Judah's family traumas. Yes, his brothers knew about his shortcomings. But there had been change in Judah and he had now taken on the leadership role of his family. Here's what the psalmist said about trying to keep our sins secret:

You have placed our iniquities before You, Our
secret sins *in the light of Your presence. (Ps. 90:8)*

Judah never knew what happened to Joseph. How did he grieve? How did he deal with the fact that it was his idea to get rid of Joseph by profiting from the sale? Money doesn't last, but secret sin has a way of haunting us for years. I am sure Judah's heart was heavy at each memory of the pain he had caused his younger brother and the pain he saw so often in the face of his aging father. He had had life change. Compassion now described his heart.

Memories of a Child Long Gone

Remember that Jacob thought he had lost Joseph to a horrible death. For twenty some years he had thought about, imagined, what Joseph would be like had he lived. Joseph was presumed dead, and it had affected Jacob to the core. Sorrow was etched in every wrinkle in his weathered brow. Tears had long gone dry. But the memories of Joseph? He held on to them with tenacity.

In talking to parents of children long gone, they still mourn. They still dream. Parents who lose a child never get over it. The pain may lessen, but it is always there. The dreams die with that child. Hope dies. Most parents who have lost a child go to their grave wondering what it would have been like had that child lived. Jacob was no exception. The ten brothers saw the grief in the countenance of their father month after month, year after year. They presumed their sin died with Joseph, for surely by now he was dead. They never got over their betrayal. They tried to bury it but now with this ruler in Egypt asking all kinds of questions. There it was, the memory, as if it had happened yesterday.

God's Orchestration of Events

Joseph saw that God had been at work in his brothers' lives. It was now obvious that God was the One who orchestrated it all. Joseph now saw the big picture and not just the pieces of the past twenty plus years. He will eventually recognize the prophecy given to Abraham about the four hundred years in slavery. He sees what is ahead for his people. But what he really saw was how God had put the pieces into place. Until now pieces of his life were scattered, not finding a place to fit. The puzzle that was his life was making sense for the first time.

Upon seeing his full brother Benjamin, it was too much for him and his emotions spilled over uncontrollably. He now "gets it" that God had brought him to Egypt, told him about the famine to come, how to solve the problem, and now his brothers had come and the lights had gone on for him. His dreams as a young man were now amazingly detailed in his mind once again.

The cupbearers dreams had been fulfilled. Pharaoh's dreams had indeed come true. God had been speaking and leading all along. He hadn't put the pieces together until his brothers came during the famine phase of the dreams. Now he realized the plan of God, and he would reveal that to them. Joseph had years to think of ways in which his brothers hurt him. How devastated he was when taken to Egypt. How cruel had been his incarceration. It was cold, dark, and damp as he was chained in the dungeons of Egypt. But God had been with him. That he now knew beyond a shadow of a doubt.

The dreams of Pharaoh got him out of prison and put him in charge of the economic health of Egypt. He was grateful. But was there an even larger plan of God? It was when his brothers bowed down to him that the lights went on. He imprisoned Simeon to "pay him back" for putting him in the pit. But God had worked on him those months while Simeon was in jail. Simeon hadn't done this! God had! God brought him to Egypt for such a time as this. God had elevated him to a position of power in order to save the lives of the very brothers who had deeply injured him. God was sovereign. Of that he knew like he had never understood before. Now here were all eleven of his brothers, together again, and Benjamin among them. The emotions overwhelmed him.

Then Joseph could not control himself before all those who stood by him, and he cried, "Have everyone go out from me." So there was no man with him when Joseph made himself known to his brothers. He wept so loudly that the Egyptians heard it, and the household of Pharaoh heard of it. Then Joseph said to his brothers, "I am Joseph! Is my father still alive?" But his brothers could not answer him, for they were dismayed at his presence.

The Power of Perspective

Then Joseph said to his brothers, "Please come closer to me." And they came closer. And he said, "I am your brother Joseph, whom you sold into Egypt. Now do not be grieved or angry with yourselves, because you sold me here, for God sent me before you to preserve life. *For the famine has been in the land these two years, and there are still five years in which there will be neither plowing nor harvesting.* God sent me before you to preserve for you a remnant in the earth, and to keep you alive by a great deliverance. Now, therefore, it was not you who sent me here, but God; *and He has made me a father to Pharaoh and lord of all his household and ruler over all the land of Egypt. (Gen. 45:1–8)*

Three times he told his brothers that God had sent him to Egypt. We are slow to get something unless we are told three times. This is here for emphasis. Joseph now understood. Would his brothers understand? No, they didn't. They were stunned. How could this be? Why is he in such a powerful position? What happened after they sold him? Oh, the questions flew! Then their thoughts took a dark turn. *"What will happen to us now?"*

Their brother was in a position of power to either help them or destroy them. Did they understand what he was saying? No, they did not. He was put in that place to keep *them* alive by giving them food? The full weight of what Joseph knew they didn't. I am sure fear was the first emotion that gripped their hearts and minds. If this is truly Joseph, will he not put us all in prison as he had done to Simeon? Would he take revenge?

Then they were thankful and talking among themselves. They still didn't know the plan Joseph was about to do for them. They didn't fully understand the sovereignty of an Almighty God who controls all things. For now, they will simply be grateful. But how could they trust him? Wouldn't he do to them what they had done to him? Amazement and fear gripped each heart as he spoke to them.

The Gift of Faith

Let's pause for a moment and talk about faith. Remember, if the character spoken of is not in the Messianic lineage, then there is another reason for including that person in the storyline of the Old Testament. As you remember, Joseph is not in the line of Christ. So why give him so much space? Could it be that he was an example of people of faith spoken of in Hebrews 11? (See appendix 3, verse 22)

Joseph had many years to wrestle with the Lord over his plight in Egypt. His faith had grown as God had shown him His plan. But that showing of God's plan was after Joseph bowed the knee and gave it all up. It was his "Lordship" conversion, when he knew God could and would do with him as He chose, when He chose, and how He chose.

That, my friends, is what we call the gift of faith. Listen to the gifts given by the Spirit of God. This applies to both Old and New Testament believers.

> *Now there are varieties of gifts, but the same Spirit. And there are varieties of ministries, and the same Lord. There are varieties of effects, but the same God who works all things in all persons. But to each one is given* the manifestation of the

Spirit for the common good. *For to one is given the word of wisdom through the Spirit, and to another the word of knowledge according to the same Spirit; to* another faith by the same Spirit, *and to another gifts of healing by the one Spirit,* (1 Cor. 12:4–9)

"Faith is a gift of the Holy Spirit (given to Joseph) for the common good of his people. It is a special gift whereby the Spirit provides believers with extraordinary confidence in God's promises, power, and presence so they can take heroic stands for the future of God's work in building His Kingdom. It is a strong, unshakable confidence in God, His Word, and His promises. Those with the gift of faith are an inspiration to their fellow believers, exhibiting a humble godliness and reliance on God's promises." (Gotquestions.org, 2015)

I believe this describes Joseph when meeting his brothers. The "light" goes on, and he remembered the dreams of his youth. He had put a quiet confidence in God, and at this point, God demonstrated to him the whys of putting him in Egypt over twenty years ago. He had grown. He had matured. He understood the plans of God for prosperity and famine. But more than that, He had a trust in the God of the Hebrews that he didn't have when young. How else could he have come up with the fact that it was God who sold him to that Ishmaelite caravan heading toward Egypt, not his brothers. How else could he have justified his untimely prison sentence and all that took place there? How else could he have understood Pharaoh's dreams and what to do about them? His faith had grown and matured. It was a quiet, humble godliness and trust in his heavenly Father. He was unshakable, not in himself but in his wholehearted trust and faith in God. He knew at this point that it wasn't about him. It wasn't about his brothers. It wasn't about prison. It wasn't about Egypt. It was all about God! God had done all of this for the sake of His Kingdom.

God had been with him, leading him, testing him, all for His glory. Joseph got it.

Now Joseph continues, *"Hurry and go up to my father, and say to him, 'Thus says your son Joseph, "God has made me lord of all Egypt; come down to me, do not delay. You shall live in the land of Goshen, and you shall be near me, you and your children and your children's children and your flocks and your herds and all that you have. There I will also provide for you, for there are still five years of famine to come, and you and your household and all that you have would be impoverished."'* (Gen. 45:9–11)

Other Spiritual Gifts of Joseph: Leadership, Administration, Discernment

Joseph did not understand as we do today that there are spiritual gifts that enhance the body of believers. Spiritual gifts are those that the Holy Spirit gives to each of us for the edification of other believers, but they are also given to glorify Him and to build His kingdom. Joseph naturally had two gifts that were demonstrated when in service to Potiphar and also while he was in prison: leadership and administration. Potiphar and the prison guard recognized these gifts when putting him in charge of other prisoners.

> *Now there are varieties of gifts, but the same Spirit. And there are varieties of ministries, and the same Lord. There are varieties of effects, but the same God who works all things in all persons. But to each one is given the manifestation of the Spirit for the common good. (1 Cor. 12:4–7)*

Joseph's discernment was noticed by Pharaoh, and because of it, he was put in a position of authority and control. Pharaoh trusted Joseph because he saw in him a leader who didn't usurp Pharaoh's authority but served under him with integrity. These spiritual gifts, along with the gift of faith, served Joseph well. He rightly used these gifts to encourage his servants, as well as Pharaoh himself. Joseph continues:

> *"Behold, your eyes see, and the eyes of my brother Benjamin see, that it is my mouth which is speaking to you. Now you must tell my father of all my splendor in Egypt, and all that you have seen; and you must hurry and bring my father down here." Then he fell on his brother Benjamin's neck and wept, and Benjamin wept on his neck. He kissed all his brothers and wept on them, and afterward his brothers talked with him. Now when the news was heard in Pharaoh's house that Joseph's brothers had come, it pleased Pharaoh and his servants. Then Pharaoh said to Joseph, "Say to your brothers, 'Do this: load your beasts and go to the land of Canaan, and take your father and your households and come to me, and I will give you the best of the land of Egypt and you will eat the fat of the land.' Now you are ordered, 'Do this: take wagons from the land of Egypt for your little ones and for your wives, and bring your father and come. Do not concern yourselves with your goods, for the best of all the land of Egypt is yours.'" Then the sons of Israel did so; and Joseph gave them wagons according to the command of Pharaoh, and gave them provisions for the journey. To each of them he gave changes of garments, but to Benjamin he gave three hundred pieces of silver and five changes of garments. To his father he sent as follows: ten*

donkeys loaded with the best things of Egypt, and
ten female donkeys loaded with grain and bread
and sustenance for his father on the journey. So
he sent his brothers away, and as they departed,
he said to them, "Do not quarrel on the journey."
(Gen. 45:12–24)

Joseph had the discernment to tell his brothers not to quarrel on the journey. Here is a younger brother telling his older brothers to be nice to each other. He senses the tension among the ten brothers. They will want to rehash their betrayal of him and rehash how on earth Joseph came to be put in a position of leadership, in Egypt no less!

Then they went up from Egypt, and came to the
land of Canaan to their father Jacob. They told
him, saying, "Joseph is still alive, and indeed he
is ruler over all the land of Egypt." But he was
stunned, for he did not believe them. When they
told him all the words of Joseph that he had spoken
to them, and when he saw the wagons that Joseph
had sent to carry him, the spirit of their father
Jacob revived. Then Israel said, "It is enough; my
son Joseph is still alive. I will go and see him before
I die." (Gen. 45:25–28)

Questions for Chapter 13

1) List your spiritual gifts (you have several). How has God used them in your life and for His glory?

2) Has there been a time in your life in which you were stunned with the twist that took place? Was it the sovereignty of God?

CHAPTER 14

THE CRESCENDO

Now do not be grieved or angry with yourselves, because you sold me here, for God sent me before you to preserve life. For the famine has been in the land these two years, and there are still five years in which there will be neither plowing nor harvesting. God sent me before you to preserve for you a remnant in the earth, and to keep you alive by a great deliverance. Now, therefore, It was not you who sent me here, but God; *and He has made me a father to Pharaoh and lord of all his household and ruler over all the land of Egypt. (Gen. 45:5-8)*

Notice that Joseph once again told the brothers three times that they did not send him to Egypt, nor enslave him, *God did.* He wanted to make very clear to his brothers that God was sovereign over everything that had happened to him since they sold him. He wasn't discounting their part in what happened, he was simply saying that God was in control with all the events leading up to his encounter with them again. He saw the big picture. They were still looking at the small piece of the puzzle that they had a part in. There are NO accidents with God. Joseph made that clear to his brothers that his being in Egypt was not an accident. It was planned by the Almighty Himself.

This passage of scripture is so powerful, not only to them, but to us thousands of years later. We too must be able to look at our life from God's perspective. He is in control, whether or not we see it, acknowledge it, talk about it, or live like it. No other passage of scripture speaks to the woundedness we all experience from time to time from another's doing. God knows exactly what He is doing in the lives of His children. The question I have to ask myself is: do I believe it?

Between this last statement and another to follow in chapter 50, we find God confirming for Jacob that He was indeed controller of all things. God simply asked Jacob not to fear for He has taken great care to provide for the entire clan of Israel by moving them to Egypt. God would provide and protect this small band of Israelites until the time He would deliver them back into the land of Canaan.

So Israel set out with all that he had, and came to Beersheba, and offered sacrifices to the God of his father Isaac. God spoke to Israel in visions of the night and said, "Jacob, Jacob." And he said, "Here I am." He said, "I am God, the God of your father; do not be afraid to go down to Egypt, for I will make you a great nation there. I will go down with you to Egypt, and I will also surely bring you up again; and Joseph will close your eyes."

Then Jacob arose from Beersheba; and the sons of Israel carried their father Jacob and their little ones and their wives in the wagons which Pharaoh had sent to carry him. They took their livestock and their property, which they had acquired in the land of Canaan, and came to Egypt, Jacob and all his descendants with him: his sons and his grandsons with him, his daughters and his granddaughters, and all his descendants he brought with him to Egypt. (Gen. 46:1-7)

Joseph prepared his chariot and went up to Goshen to meet his father Israel; as soon as he appeared before him, he fell on his neck and wept on his neck a long time. (Gen. 46:28)

The Best Land In Egypt

So Joseph settled his father and his brothers and gave them a possession in the land of Egypt, in the best of the land, in the land of Rameses, as Pharaoh had ordered. (Gen. 47:1)

The Power Of Blessing: A Healing For All Wounds

To sum up, all of you be harmonious, sympathetic, brotherly, kindhearted, and humble in spirit; not returning evil for evil or insult for insult, but giving a blessing instead; for you were called for the very purpose that you might inherit a blessing. (1 Peter 3:8-9)

Joseph turned around the "insult" that they gave him in selling him into slavery and "blessed" them instead. He gave them the *best* land in Egypt, not the worst. He gave them gifts of food, clothing, wagons and whatever else they would need to start a new life in the land of his Ephraim (future). He outdid himself in his generous spirit to them. Pharaoh came alongside him in his generosity. That's another reason I believe Pharaoh may have been a man of faith as well as Joseph.

Joseph blessed their future in accordance with his blessings. So, not only did he forgive them, honor them, love on them, he incorporated his own life into theirs. He and his sons became part of the ongoing generations of Israelites in the land of Egypt. Many years later the twelve tribes (not eleven) would all be released from the bondage that enslaved them. They were family. Families can wound. But families can heal. One person has to be the Joseph in the family. They have to become the forgiver and let God be the healer.

The principle of love and blessing works every time. For an insult, we need to return a blessing. God promises to bless us when we do this. Joseph is a clear example of the Messiah in what he did for his brothers. They had sold him into slavery. Because of it he had spent years in prison. When he saw them he could have easily given an insult for an insult. He could have put them in prison and thrown away the key. What he did instead was to bless the socks off them. This was a spiritual decision on his part. It wasn't human. It was a God-thing.

We see a brother not returning insult for insult or evil for evil but instead giving something they were incapable of earning, working for, or even desiring. The best land in Egypt and wagons for their journey. Clothes they didn't buy. Food they couldn't grow. He didn't just give them food – that would have been wonderful in and of itself. He gave and gave and gave. He gave in the midst of the great depression that all lands were experiencing. They wouldn't have to stand in food lines. They were blessed beyond their understanding. The land he gave was productive. They would not go hungry. They would have houses and crops – and all of that was given – not because they deserved it, but because they did NOT. They had done NOTHING to warrant what Joseph gave. They hadn't asked for it. They hadn't dreamt about it. They hadn't prayed about it. They hadn't given one thought to inheriting such an astounding gift.

> *For you have been called for this purpose, since Christ also suffered for you, leaving you an example for you to follow in His steps, who committed no sin, nor was any deceit found in His mouth; and while being reviled, He did not revile in return; while suffering, He uttered no threats, but kept entrusting Himself to Him who judges righteously; and He Himself bore our sins in His body on the cross, so that we might die to sin and live to righteousness; for by His wounds you were healed. For you were continually straying like sheep, but now you have returned to the Shepherd and Guardian of your souls. (1 Peter 2:21-25)*

Why is Joseph often spoken of as a "type" of Christ? Jesus not only died for our sins, He gave us a life free of the worry of perishing. Then He gave us Heaven!!! And then He will give us the New Earth where we will have no worries, no sin, no tears or heartache. Clothes that won't wear out. Bodies that won't grow old. Minds that will not deteriorate. Our every need met. He promises the best land for our every need – for eternity. And we stand astounded!

The Brothers Again Question

After the death of their father, Jacob, we have another outstanding comment from Joseph and a poignant lesson for us.

> *When Joseph's brothers saw that their father was dead, they said, "What if Joseph bears a grudge*

against us and pays us back in full for all the wrong which we did to him!" So they sent a message to Joseph, saying, "Your father charged before he died, saying, 'Thus you shall say to Joseph, "Please forgive, I beg you, the transgression of your brothers and their sin, for they did you wrong."' And now, please forgive the transgression of the servants of the God of your father." And Joseph wept when they spoke to him. (Gen. 50:15-17)

The brothers still didn't comprehend Joseph's words to them. Joseph understood the sovereignty of an Almighty God who holds the whole world in His hands. He controls seasons. He controls nations and families. He controls family's moves from one nation to the next, from one town to the next, and from one house to the next. He controls how many children come into each family. He controls riches and poverty. He controls destinies. He controls emotions and feelings. Joseph understood and acknowledged the sovereignty of God.

His brothers accept it, but they don't "get it." They still feared Joseph would punish them when their father died. That's why Joseph cried. What did he have to do in order for them to understand? He could do nothing more except in action for the rest of their lives. He gave them land. He gave them money. He honored his father and their mothers. He honored family.

Am I In God's Place Of Judge And Jury?

Then his brothers also came and fell down before him and said, "Behold, we are your servants." But Joseph said to them, "do not be afraid, for am I in God's place? As for you, you meant evil against

> me, but God meant it for good *in order to bring*
> *about this present result, to preserve many people*
> *alive. So therefore, do not be afraid; I will provide*
> *for you and your little ones." So he comforted them*
> *and spoke kindly to them. (Gen. 50:18-21)*

This is one of the most poignant statements in all of Scripture. This passage is quoted more than any other when dealing with wounds and the sovereignty of the Almighty. By this one statement you and I can believe that God orchestrates the trials He brings into our lives for two reasons: for our good and for His glory. I dare say if I had not gone through the trials in my life that I have I wouldn't understand this powerful passage. God knows just how to preserve my life and the lives of others He places around me.

Joseph told them God had orchestrated the whole of their story. Joseph would NOT sit as judge (am I in God's place) in their lives. What they did (their sin), they had to live with. What Joseph did was bless them instead of cursing them. He became "Christ" in their lives. He forgave. He blessed. He honored. He loved. His perspective was God's perspective. He was able to look beyond humanity to God who does all things well.

I am amazed that there is no indication in Scripture that any of the brothers ever asked for forgiveness, personally. They instead sent a message they had written for Jacob asking for forgiveness (Gen. 50:16-17). Not one came directly to him and asked for forgiveness. Joseph never demanded their asking for forgiveness. God shows us that Joseph left the judging to the Father, who is a good Judge and judges rightly. Joseph took the high road and blessed anyway. He gave the best, not the worst (they didn't deserve any land). Joseph forgave. Period. He let the past go (Manasseh) so that the future (Ephraim) looked bright for the entire family. But it is amazing to me that NONE of the brothers pleaded with him for mercy and forgiveness.

When Joseph told the brothers he would not sit as Judge over them he was in essence putting the ball in their court for God, the righteous Judge, to deal with their individual hearts. God knows how to deal with us – and with everyone else. God doesn't absolve us from forgiving our offender. He simply asks us to forgive and leave the judging and the sentence up to God. It's easy to forgive a small offense, but one that has taken place over years is more difficult and will take more time for healing and perspective.

Healing can only begin when the "idea" of forgiveness begins. It's not easy and it's certainly not "fair", but it is the only way God deals with our hearts. None of us are sinless. God knows how to work in each and every individual involved. God asks us to forgive, no matter what, even if we are not asked for forgiveness from the other person. We may never get an apology. We may never get, "I was wrong." That's not for us to judge or require. It's great if people do ask for our forgiveness, but God doesn't want us to wait for that to happen before we forgive.

God is the only One who knows how to take what Satan means for evil and turn it around for good. We simply do not know how to turn it around. What we sometimes think of as a setback may indeed be God's way to take us to the next level. God's plan will always be right. It will always lean toward justice. We can believe lies told to us or done to us, or we can believe that a good God gave us trials to make us stronger and more mature.

We must understand that our lives are being orchestrated by an unseen hand. God is causing *all things* to work together for good for those of us who have put our faith in Him. We may not understand at any given moment the plan and purpose of God in our lives. But as we begin to put the pieces of our own lives together (both good and hurtful) and we see God's movement, we begin to understand that our life isn't about us. It's all about Him. We were designed for a purpose and that purpose is to glorify God. Period. God will take us through an individual plan (my plan won't look like your plan) to bring us to the ultimate statement that Joseph came to: God meant it for good for me and He also meant what I experience, difficult as it may be, for preservation purposes. There is no other way to look at hard times in our lives.

God doesn't want us to sit as judge and jury concerning anyone else's faults, weaknesses or sin. We are not in God's place as judge and we will not make decisions for anyone else's life as a jury does. God is a Judge who does right. He is also the jury and He will determine the outcome, not only for my life but anyone who injures me. His justice will be right. His verdict will be right. Anytime I find myself judging another person's motives I am in the jury box. God doesn't want me there. He wants me to leave justice up to Him and Him alone to resolve in His timing.

> For He Himself has said, "I will never desert you, nor will I ever forsake you," so that we confidently say, "The Lord is my helper, I will not be afraid. What will man do to me?" (Hebrews 13:5-6)

God always has our back. He will not leave us. Therefore, we can be assured that in His timing and in His way (which always redeems) He will take care of the people who have wounded us. (In some instances I am the one who has done the wounding). Joseph knew God would deal with his brothers, not him. God would deal with anyone else in Joseph's life who had wounded him. At this point, Joseph simply left judge and jury up to Him who judges righteously. And that is the task we have before us. Are we willing to let God be God in someone else's life? I don't have to take revenge. I don't have to manipulate God. God knows perfectly well how to do it, when to do it and why do it. We simply do not.

The thing He continues to ask of us is to forgive, whether the person has asked for it or not. We are not to say, "I will forgive, when they ask for it." Or "I will forgive when they become convicted of their sin." God has not left that open to us. If I want to be forgiven, I must forgive. Forgiveness in scripture is conditional.

For if you forgive others for their transgressions, your heavenly Father will also forgive you. But if you do not forgive others, then your Father will not forgive your transgressions. (Matt. 6:14-15)

Seventy Times Seven

Jesus was asked by Peter how many times we are to forgive those who wound us and then asked if seven was enough (which is a perfect number). Jesus then replied,

Jesus said to him, "I do not say to you, up to seven times, but up to seventy times seven. (Matt. 18:22)

As you can see, Jesus told Peter to forgive 490 times. By then who's counting? We count one wound and keep on counting that same wound over and over again. We "feel" like we have been wounded 490 times! The issue of forgiveness is innumerable. How many sins do I have? Innumerable. How many sins has Jesus forgiven on the cross? Innumerable. How many sins have been committed against me? One, two, ten? How many do I need to forgive? Innumerable. This passage is not about eternal life. Our sins have been forgiven at the cross – all of them. When we become a believer in Christ we are bound for heaven and all that entails. This passage is about our heart. Notice the passage below and the amazing last sentence.

"For this reason the kingdom of heaven may be compared to a king who wished to settle accounts with his slaves. When he had begun to settle them, one who owed him ten thousand talents was brought to him. But since he did not have the means to repay, his lord commanded him to be sold, along with his wife and children and all that he had, and repayment to be made. So the slave fell to the ground and prostrated himself before him, saying, 'Have patience with me and I will repay you everything.' And the lord of that slave felt compassion and released him and forgave him the debt. But that slave went out and found one of his fellow slaves who owed him a hundred denarii; and he seized him and began to choke him, saying, 'Pay back what you owe.' So his fellow slave fell to the ground and began to plead with him, saying, 'Have patience with me and I will repay you.' But he was unwilling and went and threw him in prison until he should pay back what was owed. So when his fellow slaves saw what had happened, they were deeply grieved and came and reported to their lord all that had happened. Then summoning him, his lord said to him, 'You wicked slave, I forgave you all that debt because you pleaded with me. Should you not also have had mercy on your fellow slave, in the same way that I had mercy on you?' And his lord, moved with anger, handed him over to the torturers until he should repay all that was owed him. My heavenly Father will also do the same to you, if each of you does not forgive from your heart." *(Matt. 18:23-35)*

Why does forgiveness work miracles in our lives? Because we are all guilty of wounding others. If we ever want anyone else to let us off the hook when we are the one doing the wounding, we must realize we need to let others off the hook too, difficult as it may be. They don't deserve to be let off. But do we? It's easy to see the sin in someone else's life but we are sometimes blind concerning our own shortcomings. That's why we are asked by God to let Him deal with our offender. He knows how to win the other person to Himself. We push them away. He pulls them to Him. He sees the heart of others, we cannot. He sees the timing it's going to take in their hearts. He sees what He has to take them through to get their attention. He sees that in us as well. Can we let go and let God do His job?

Results Of Not Forgiving = Inner Torment

What does an unforgiving spirit do in us? We experience a bitter heart and negative attitude toward those who wounded us. Our heart becomes so cancerous that we are hard to live with. We spout words like, "I would have never done that to him/her!" We can't say that because we are all capable of hurting others as we have been hurt. I wonder if in prison Joseph saw his own heart and that he too was capable of rejecting one or more of his brothers. Was he capable of gaining money to wound one of them? Was he too, capable of murder? Was he capable of falsely accusing another? Was he capable of forgetting to help a friend in need? God spoke to his heart in those two years in prison when he had to come to grips with his own sinfulness.

If in times of wounding that you received from another, there have been harsh words spoken to or of that person, asking forgiveness of your sin is worth the conversation. We must "own" our own sin, whatever that is. You don't need to apologize for the wrong done to you. That is up to the other person. But if you want your slate to be clean, then asking for forgiveness might be in order. This will help the healing begin on both sides. You will know in your heart when this needs to be done.

Joseph demonstrated that not only had he forgiven his brothers, he had put them squarely in the court of the Almighty to deal with them and to forgive them and to draw them to Himself. *He took his hands off so that God could keep His hands on!* He forgave and then dropped it. His actions then spoke volumes to his extended family.

People Are Watching

When we harbor bitterness in our hearts it shows on the outside. Our children are watching how we go through the wounding process and how we come out the other side. If the wounding is severe, we may indeed sound like Mrs. Job when she said, "Just curse God and die!" At times we feel just like she felt. We need not be hard on her, for at times the pain is so great we just *want* to die. (Remember Job and Mrs. Job lost ten children in one day!) God sees and hears and understands and at those times He simply puts His loving arms around us to comfort and begin the healing process. We may not even be able to pray because our pain is too great. God was not hard on Mrs. Job and He will not be hard on us either. (She's gotten a bad rap all these years). He was kind to her. He understood her. He made her. He knew it would take some time for her to come around. Job came around quickly. For Mrs. Job it took longer. When it comes to children it always seems to take longer for the woman to come through the healing process. God will be kind to us and will bring us through our pain to experience healing and restoration.

Our children are especially vulnerable to our attitude when we are wounded. They see and they hear. We must be careful to teach them when we finally get through our own healing. Raising children to be unforgiving is one of the worst things we can do to them. They then become bitter and unforgiving people.

Friends are also watching. When we spew hatred and bitterness they see. But good friends will pray for our healing and health. That's what it means when it says in Proverbs 18:24, "*a friend sticks closer than a brother*". Make sure you are supporting your friends who are going through trials. They will more likely support you when you go through trials.

The Beauty Of The Wounding Process

The beauty of this story is that you and I can become like Joseph. It's in our realm of thinking that when we are tried by the wounding process, when we have wrestled with God, we find we are inadequate to meet the wounding head on. We then lay it down and let God be God in our lives. We too can say with Joseph "*They meant it for evil but God meant it for good in my life.*" Therefore I will not question the "why's" of what I go through. He wounds and He also heals.

Jesus too was wounded. He was wounded by his friends whom he taught and lived with for three years. He was wounded by His culture surrounding Him. Some in His family forsook Him. He was wounded by the religious people of His time. But it is through His wounding that you and I are healed. We are healed of our attitudes, our bitterness, our blaming others. We are healed of all the sin in our lives, confessed and unconfessed, known and unknown. He died for us so that we are presented to the Father without sin. Wow!

> *But He was pierced through for our transgressions,*
> *He was crushed for our iniquities;*
> *The chastening for our well-being fell upon Him,*
> *And by His scourging we are healed. (Isaiah 53:5)*

The Marvelous Name Of Joseph

Because I believe biblical names are important (Introductory chapter), I feel it is fitting to end this book with two names that are pregnant with meaning: Joseph and Benjamin. Let's unpack their names in light of this story and the effect they have on our story in the twenty-first century.

Rachel named her first son Joseph, saying, *"You have taken away my reproach"*. His new name meant, *" He will add, or increase"*. Joseph's name takes on the characteristic of the cross of Jesus the Messiah. Reproach means disapproval or disgrace. When Jesus died on the cross He took away my disgrace, my sin, my disapproval and made me whole so that I can inherit eternal life with my Creator. When Joseph told his brothers that it was God who had done this and not them, he was taking away their reproach, their sin, their disgrace. Because the name means increase and add, Jesus has always been in the process of adding to and increasing numbers for His Kingdom. Those words also take on what Jesus does in our lives: He increases joy through the pain we go through in life. Your life and mine have never been the same since Jesus entered our hearts. Truly we have been "added to" in ways we will not even comprehend till we are with Him eternally.

Joseph has always remained in historical records as a "type" of Christ in that he was able to remove from his brothers their disgrace. He was also the one who "spoke" life into their damaged egos. They too would increase in numbers but also in the blessings given to the whole of Israel. Joseph demonstrated blessing and abundant living to his family, the same that Christ does to us, His children, His family. Joseph gave from his untold riches so that his brothers would have abundance. What a picture of Christ.

In Deuteronomy 33:13-17, the tribe of Joseph is blessed by Moses. He is given the choice things of heaven and earth and is crowned with distinction among his brothers. Not only has the reproach been taken away but honor has been added.

The Equally Marvelous Name Of Benjamin

When Rachel she lay dying at the birth of her second son she wanted to name him Benoni (son of my sorrow), but Jacob intervened and named him, Benjamin, *"Son of my right hand"*. Prophetically this is another position given to the Son of Man by God the Father. It refers to a position of reigning and ruling. Listen to these verses:

> *But from now on the Son of Man will be seated at the right hand of the power of God." (Luke 22:69)*

> *Jesus said, "I am; and you shall see the Son of Man sitting at the right hand of Power, and coming with the clouds of heaven." (Mark 14:62)*

> *The Lord says to my Lord: "Sit at My right hand Until I make Your enemies a footstool for Your feet." (Psalm 110:1)*

> *Jesus said to him, "You have said it yourself; nevertheless I tell you, hereafter you will see the Son of Man sitting at the right hand of Power, and coming on the clouds of heaven." (Matt. 26:64)*

> *Fixing our eyes on Jesus, the author and perfecter of faith, who for the joy set before Him endured the cross, despising the shame, and has sat down at the right hand of the throne of God. (Hebrews 12:2)*

Before his death, Moses blessed each of the tribes. He said of Benjamin:

"He (Benjamin) dwells between His shoulders"
(Deuteronomy 33:12)

Benjamin means security (dwelling between the shoulders) for the believer. It also means reigning in power for the Messiah who was to come.

Isn't it interesting that God gives names when we are in the womb? He gave Joseph a name which is the one of the main characteristics of the Messiah. He further gives names like Benjamin to instill in all of us what He has done for us in coming to earth, living as a human, dying on a cruel cross, and ascending to Heaven where He now sits, waiting for the day when He will stand and welcome us home. Names are indeed important to God. He chooses names for us and He chooses names for Himself. Names tell stories if we will but listen to their meaning.

Summarizing The Book

The question I posed at the beginning of the book was: How was God going to take an arrogant seventeen-year old boy and make him into the man of God we find at the end of the story? That's the question I hope has been answered.

God took a cocky seventeen-year old boy, gave him dreams for the future and proceeded to take him through a series of trials that would crush his arrogance, build his character, and cause him to look to Him who is sovereign over all things.

God used the jealousy of ten older brothers, who wanted nothing more than to be free from the young pride of teen life. God needed to take Joseph out of his dysfunctional family so he could learn to stand alone and become a mature man whose hope was in God alone.

The trials made him stronger. He had to quit looking back and quit looking around for someone to rescue him. There was good in the hurts heaped upon him. There was good in the prison sentence. There was good in his wrestling with an Almighty God. There was good in God allowing pain.

It's okay to question God. It's okay to struggle. It's okay to momentarily want revenge. But it's *not okay* to stay there. We must move past the hurt to knowing that what Satan means for evil, God means for good.

The question before us is the same. How has God, in His sovereignty, taken me from my teen years to become the person I hope I have become? He did it the same way He did for Joseph. Do you see that? I have been through more pain than I would care to enumerate to get to where I am today. Do I still struggle? Did Joseph struggle as an old man? Probably. I am sure God wasn't done with him just because his story ends when he was in his forties. Did he go through more pain in his life? To answer that question, have you? God is not finished with any of us till we stand before Him, having run our race of faith and finished our course.

Through the names of Joseph's sons he is sharing his testimony. God expects of us to dig into His Word, unlocking it's mysteries. It's not about us. It's all about Him. He preordained that you and I would be on this earth for one purpose: to give Him glory. He will take us through the depths of trials to mold us into the very image of Himself. For most of us it takes years to figure out what He is doing. When we begin to understand that God wants the glory for whatever trials we go through, we can go through them, not unscathed, but for our good. We are humbled through trials. Good times don't necessarily bring out the "God-consciousness" in us. It's the hard times that do this. We are never thankful for the trials we have to endure. But I dare say, we are better human beings after experiencing the wounding that comes through trials. We don't pray for wounding, it comes anyway. We certainly don't pray for pain. Every trial, every hurt comes to our hearts through the good heart of the Father.

Jesus stands as our Advocate. He intercedes for us when we are too wounded even to pray.

Praise God He has left us with an incredible story of woundedness. He actually didn't finish the story of Joseph. We want to know, "did any of the brothers repent"? Did any of them personally ask for forgiveness? That's not for us to know. God has left the pages blank – only we can fill them in in our own lives. What are we going to do with our pain and wounds? Remember, we are wounded by the people we love, not by those we do not love. We are wounded in the places where we found fulfillment, not in the places we do not. God is in the wounding. He is also in the healing. Are we going to give it to our heavenly Judge? If we do, He takes it, nails it to the cross and begins the healing process. And that's what we want – healing from the wounds of life. He is an amazing God!

Two Trains Of Thought In Scripture

In the beginning of this book we talked about two lines of thought running through Old Testament history. The whole Bible is all about the Messiah, both Old, leading up to His coming, and New, the fulfillment of His coming. The Old Testament is the unfolding of the Messianic line: His lineage, His purpose, and Satan's attacks on that blood-line.

We also mentioned that throughout Old Testament history, God stops and tells the stories of people of faith. Joseph's life is a one of maturing faith and a God-perspective that is second to none. His story is the kind that when we are running our own race in our era of time, he steps from the side-lines to hand us a cup of cold water. That cup is filled with encouragement that when times are tough and we have been wounded to the core, his story teaches us how to view hurt and trials and hard times.

No wonder this fantastic story is one of the most loved in all of Scripture. It is told in numerous ways, by countless people, in every era of time. Joseph came to the conclusion that we too must come to: it's not about me. It's all about *HIM*.

Dear reader, this story is a story of our lives. We want the fairy tale ending. But first there is the struggle. There is humiliation. There is pain. And it's when we stop the wrestling match with God and bow the knee that He shows us how much He loves us and how He has been with us the whole time, walking beside us in the pain and anguish of life.

Are we of the opinion that when Joseph passed the four tests mentioned in this book that his life was smooth sailing from that time forward? Did he ever experience the pain of woundedness again I wonder? If he was like you and me, and he was, then the answer is yes. Even during the time of writing this book, I have experienced wounding again in my life. Am I exempt? No and neither are you. Trials and woundedness sometimes come out of left field especially when we are most vulnerable. When did Joseph finish with testing and being wounded? Age 110!!! When will I finish? When my life is over and I am so ready to be with the Lord.

None of us want a Manasseh. We don't want to keep forgiving. God has not left that option open to us. We all want an Ephraim, a bright future. But first we must have a Manasseh. We must, from the heart, forgive those who have wounded us in the past and in the future wounds, of which there may be a few more to go. Jesus said – forgive as you have been forgiven. We can't live in the wounds. We will put them away so that we can live in the high calling of Christ Jesus. He paid it all. Can we not surrender?

In closing, do you understand why some stories in the Bible take on such meaning? Joseph is not in the Messianic lineage, yet his story is powerful beyond our comprehension. Why? Because it is the story of me and the story of you. Wounding is part of the human condition. Through this story we are much more aware that we wound others and that we get wounded by others. It's the story of us.

In the names of Joseph and Benjamin is the gospel. Both names signify what Jesus did on the cross for us. He took my sins, my reproach, my dysfunction and nailed them to the cross. Having died for our sins once for all, He arose and is now seated at the right hand of the Father and forever became our Advocate. He paid the penalty for my sins and because He is the Judge, the Jury and my Advocate, I have been made flawless by His blood.

The story of Joseph is the Gospel. "Satan meant it unto evil but God means it for our good." We, who were a people far off, have been brought near. We were in deep poverty. We were in agony. We have been burdened with our own sin and guilt. Jesus, by a great deliverance, rescues us from our lives of poverty, nails our wounds and our sins to His cross, and then goes to prepare a place for us beyond our wildest aspirations in a city called the New Jerusalem.

> *"Things which eye has not seen and ear has not heard, And which have not entered the heart of man, All that God has prepared for those who love Him." 1 Corinthians 2:9*

That my friends, is Good News!

The Lion and The Lamb

He's coming on the clouds
Kings and kingdoms will bow down
And every chain will break
As broken hearts declare His praise
For who can stop The Lord almighty
CHORUS
Our God is the Lion
The Lion of Judah
He's roaring with power
And fighting our battles
And every knee will bow before Him
Our God is the Lamb
The Lamb that was slain
For the sin of the world
His blood breaks the chains
And every knee will bow before the Lion and the Lamb
Every knee will bow before the Lion and the Lamb
So open up the gates
Make way before the King of Kings
Our God who comes to save
Is here to set the captives free
For who can stop the Lord Almighty

QUESTIONS FOR CHAPTER 14

1) In this book we talked about three areas of wounding: family, workplace, and friendship. Joseph never required of his brothers to ask for forgiveness. Why? What did he do instead?

2) Have you, from your heart, forgiven those who have wounded you?

3) Write the steps you have done to forgive and put the past away. If you are still holding onto grudges, woundedness and pain, can you finally let go?

4) Are there steps you need to take to talk to someone who has wounded you?

5) Are there people you need to go to, to ask their forgiveness?

6) Have you asked forgiveness for your part in the wounding process (harsh words, language, name-calling, etc?)

7) Have you begun to pray for blessing for those who have wounded you?

EPILOGUE

Jacob Blessed Ephraim And Manasseh
(in place of Joseph – double blessing)

I imagine Joseph's sons, Manasseh and Ephraim, enjoyed getting to know their cousins and the large extended family. They became "Hebrews" and enjoyed their uncles and aunts and grandfather. Finally they could openly worship the God of their father, Joseph. They were young children when the extended family came to live among them. They got to ride on Josephs' chariot, but they got to eat and play among their relatives' families. What an interesting childhood they must have had. Joseph was proud of his Hebrew identity. I am sure these two boys also played with Egyptian friends. But as they grew they identified with the people of God, the Hebrews. At the death of their grandfather, Jacob, they were blessed as sons of Israel for they were Israelites indeed.

> *Now your two sons, who were born to you in the land of Egypt before I came to you in Egypt, are mine; Ephraim and Manasseh shall be mine, as Reuben and Simeon are. (Israelites) When Israel saw Joseph's sons, he said, "Who are these?" Joseph said to his father, "They are my sons, whom God has given me here." So he said, "Bring them to me,*

please, that I may bless them." Joseph took them both, Ephraim with his right hand toward Israel's left, and Manasseh with his left hand toward Israel's right, and brought them close to him. But Israel stretched out his right hand and laid it on the head of Ephraim, who was the younger, and his left hand on Manasseh's head, crossing his hands, although Manasseh was the firstborn. He blessed Joseph, and said, "The God before whom my fathers Abraham and Isaac walked, The God who has been my shepherd all my life to this day, The angel who has redeemed me from all evil, Bless the lads; And may my name live on in them, And the names of my fathers Abraham and Isaac; And may they grow into a multitude in the midst of the earth." When Joseph saw that his father laid his right hand on Ephraim's head, it displeased him; and he grasped his father's hand to remove it from Ephraim's head to Manasseh's head. Joseph said to his father, "Not so, my father, for this one is the firstborn. Place your right hand on his head." But his father refused and said, "I know, my son, I know; he also will become a people and he also will be great. However, his younger brother shall be greater than he, and his descendants shall become a multitude of nations." He blessed them that day, saying, "By you Israel will pronounce blessing, saying, 'May God make you like Ephraim and Manasseh!" "Thus he put Ephraim before Manasseh (Gen. 48:5-20)

Jacob gave Joseph the double portion normally reserved for the eldest son. You will see in the blessings to his twelve sons that Reuben had been removed from the double blessing because of his sin of sleeping with his father's concubine, Bilhah (Genesis 35:22) Jacob took away the double blessing from Reuben and gave it to Joseph's two sons, Ephraim and Manasseh. These two sons would inherit land centuries later in Canaan. (There is no land that would be allocated to Joseph but he would get double land through Manasseh and Ephraim. See Appendix Two for the blessings of the twelve sons.)

Death Of Jacob

Then he charged them and said to them, "I am about to be gathered to my people; bury me with my fathers in the cave that is in the field of Ephron the Hittite, in the cave that is in the field of Machpelah, which is before Mamre, in the land of Canaan, which Abraham bought along with the field from Ephron the Hittite for a burial site. There they buried Abraham and his wife Sarah, there they buried Isaac and his wife Rebekah, and there I buried Leah— the field and the cave that is in it, purchased from the sons of Heth." When Jacob finished charging his sons, he drew his feet into the bed and breathed his last, and was gathered to his people. (Gen. 49:29-33)

So Joseph went up to bury his father, and with him went up all the servants of Pharaoh, the elders of his household and all the elders of the land of Egypt, and all the household of Joseph and his brothers and his father's household; they left only their little ones and their flocks and their herds in the land of Goshen. (Gen. 50:7-8)

Death Of Joseph (age 110)

Now Joseph stayed in Egypt, he and his father's household, and Joseph lived one hundred and ten years. Joseph saw the third generation of Ephraim's sons; also the sons of Machir, the son of Manasseh, were born on Joseph's knees. Joseph said to his brothers, "I am about to die, but God will surely take care of you and bring you up from this land to the land which He promised on oath to Abraham, to Isaac and to Jacob."

Then Joseph made the sons of Israel swear, saying, "God will surely take care of you, and you shall carry my bones up from here." So Joseph died at the age of one hundred and ten years; and he was embalmed and placed in a coffin in Egypt. (Gen. 50:22-26)

Joseph's bones were preserved and embalmed like Jacob's (50:2)

Their Sojourn In Egypt Before The Exodus

Before Joseph ever came to Egypt God knew there would be a famine in the known world. Drought would come. Crops would be obliterated. Food would be scarce. Egypt was a ruling power and could help the rest of the known world. Israel was a fledgling group of unknown people, nomads without a home. They had increased to a small group of about 70. Since they were not powerful, the famine could wipe them out. The story of Judah and Tamar (Genesis 38) had already occurred, producing twin sons, one of whom was slated to carry on the lineage of the Messiah. Israel's family clans had to be protected so they could grow and increase in number. God's purpose was to surround and protect this fledgling tribe of Hebrews. His hand had been upon Abraham and his descendants. He would now put them in a cocoon to grow and flourish. But it wouldn't be in Canaan.

There had also been a prophecy given to Abraham that the people who came after him would be enslaved in a different land.

> *God said to Abram, "Know for certain that your descendants will be strangers in a land that is not theirs, where they will be enslaved and oppressed four hundred years. But I will also judge the nation whom they will serve, and afterward they will come out with many possessions. (Gen. 15:13-14)*

Joseph never fully identified with the Egyptians and their gods. He retained his identity and his sons would do likewise. Moses would be like him – Moses would remember Joseph and would bring his people out of bondage.

Did the Hebrew people ever wonder about that prophecy? If they did, it must have been on the back burner of their minds, not something they talked about. But God had a timetable to fulfill. He had given that prophecy to Abraham and time was on the march. He needed to get His people to Egypt. Why Egypt? He could have brought them all at the same time. But instead He needed one who would be placed in a position of authority in order for blessing and preservation purposes. By the time the brothers came Joseph understood the prophecy and why Egypt had been chosen.

Egypt had unwritten or maybe even written laws that said you could not intermarry with foreigners. You couldn't eat at the same table, you surely couldn't sleep with them and have children. So, God, wanting the Hebrew people to remain pure knew that they would not be intermarrying in Egypt. Not because the Hebrew people had a taboo but because Egypt did. The brothers in Canaan had already started intermarrying into Canaan. God needed to take them out, protect their lineage, and keep them pure. They were unable to do that because they weren't yet following Yahweh wholeheartedly. They were few in number and so were taking wives among the people where they lived. God had to remove them.

Throughout the Old Testament times God was always protecting the Messianic lineage. Judah and his family would be among those protected people. They needed to multiply. Hadn't He told Abraham that they would be a mighty people and that Canaan would be their promised land? That had not happened yet. There was work to be done. He had to place these Hebrew people in a position of teachability and trainability. They had to know how to serve and how to lead. Yes, there was coming a time in which they would be huge in numbers and training in obedience was necessary for the future. In the midst of that huge number of people the Messianic line would be safe from the wiles of Satan or anyone else who would want to destroy "the seed". The "seed" (genealogy of Messiah) would be protected by Egypt although years of slavery were in their corporate future as a nation.

God sent Joseph to Egypt, not to Assyria, nor Saudi Arabia, nor Edom or Moab. He placed Joseph among the rulers of Egyptian culture. God placed Joseph in a position that would either make or break him spiritually. It was harsh, but it would be complete in teaching him faith in the promised "seed" that was to come. The promised Redeemer was muted theology at this point but it was unmistakably there in the stories and genealogy that was passed down to this family of Hebrews. Joseph knew the prophecies. And he believed. He had faith in this "unseen" God who would bring to pass His plans.

What kept Joseph on track? He knew, understood and believed the promises of God to Abraham, Isaac and Jacob. He put his faith in the God of his Fathers. God also needed to protect the Messianic lineage from harm – satanic or human – so He sent Joseph on ahead to prepare the way and to give them a wonderful piece of land to farm and raise their families. God would protect them and keep their Hebrew blood-line pure.

Their sojourn was to be temporary until God was ready to bring them out as a very large number, to go back into Canaan to conquer and live there. Had they not become slaves, they would have never wanted to leave. Ever. So God had to place them in slavery so they would cry out to Him for a Redeemer. They needed one in the flesh in their time of need and that person became Moses. They would often cry out in their inner being for a permanent Redeemer. That time would come. But not yet….

Moses And The Exodus

When it came time for Moses to bring this huge number of Israelites out of Egypt Joseph had asked them to bring his bones with them. The tribe of Ephraim would have been assigned that task. There was a young man from that tribe who would be the "keeper of the bones" and he would bring them with he and his family. That man's name was Joshua. He would be one of two men who were born in Egypt, would travel around the wilderness for forty years and have the privilege of going into the land of Canaan to conquer it and live there. He would bury Joseph's bones in the land allotted by God to Ephraim.

> *Now they buried the bones of Joseph, which the sons of Israel brought up from Egypt, at Shechem, in the piece of ground which Jacob had bought from the sons of Hamor the father of Shechem for*

one hundred pieces of money; and they became the inheritance of Joseph's sons. (Josh. 24"32)

The City Of Shechem Today

The city of Shechem, positioned in a pass between the mountains of Gerizim and Eibal and controlling the Askar Plains to the east, was an important regional center more than 3,500 years ago. As the existing remains show, it lay within fortifications of massive stones, was entered through monumental gates and centered on a temple with walls five yards (meters) thick. (online quote about Shechem)

NABLUS, West Bank (AP) — Archaeologists unearthing a biblical ruin inside a Palestinian city in the West Bank are writing the latest chapter in a 100-year-old excavation that has been interrupted by two world wars and numerous rounds of Mideast upheaval. Working on an urban lot that long served residents of Nablus as an unofficial dump for garbage and old car parts, Dutch and Palestinian archaeologists are learning more about the ancient city of Shechem, and opened the site to the public as an archaeological park in the year 2012.

Archeology Today

Viewing the recent (May 12, 2016) television special on National Religious Broadcasters, called: *"Beyond Patterns of Evidence: he Exodus,"*

archeologists have now uncovered in the area of Goshen (Ramses) in Egypt, a Semitic village. It's called "Evidence at Avaris". It is a large village of Semitic population dating back to the 12th dynasty. The middle house, is surrounded by 12 pillars, and 11 graves surround that main house with one tomb unearthed in the shape of a small pyramid. There are no bones but there is a demolished statue of an Egyptian within that pyramid. This tomb is surrounded by Semitic houses and grave-sites. Proof cannot be determined as no names have been unearthed that say "Joseph" or "Zephenath." But an Egyptian tomb in the midst of Semitic graves? Very strange unless......

It's a probability that Joseph lived and died among his brothers and their families. Canaanite pottery has been unearthed. The homes unearthed are "four room houses" – definitely not Egyptian but Semitic. It's the first tangible evidence that the story of Joseph and his brothers is true from an archeology standpoint.

The Tribes (Sons) Who Came to Egypt

(Genesis 46:8–26)

Now these are the names of the sons of Israel, *Jacob and his sons, who went to Egypt:*

Sons of Leah

    Reuben, Jacob's firstborn.

    The sons of *Reuben*: Hanoch and Pallu and Hezron and Carmi.

    The sons of *Simeon*: Jemuel and Jamin and Ohad and Jachin and Zohar and Shaul, the son of a Canaanite woman.

    The sons of *Levi*: Gershon, Kohath, and Merari.

    The sons of *Judah*: (Er and Onan deceased) and Shelah and Perez and Zerah). And the sons of Perez were Hezron and Hamul.

    The sons of *Issachar*: Tola and Puvvah and Iob and Shimron.

    The sons of *Zebulun*: Sered and Elon and Jahleel.

    These are the sons of Leah, whom she bore to Jacob in Paddan-aram, with his daughter Dinah; all his sons and his daughters *numbered* thirty-three.

Sons of Zilpah

The sons of *Gad*: Ziphion and Haggi, Shuni and Ezbon, Eri and Arodi and Areli.

The sons of *Asher*: Imnah and Ishvah and Ishvi and Beriah and their sister Serah. And the sons of Beriah: Heber and Malchiel.

These are the sons of Zilpah, whom Laban gave to his daughter Leah; and she bore to Jacob these sixteen persons.

Sons of Rachel

The *sons of Jacob's wife Rachel*: Joseph and Benjamin. Now to *Joseph* in the land of Egypt were born Manasseh and Ephraim, whom Asenath, the daughter of Potiphera, priest of On, bore to him.

The sons of *Benjamin*: Bela and Becher and Ashbel, Gera and Naaman, Ehi and Rosh, Muppim and Huppim and Ard.

These are the sons of Rachel, who were born to Jacob; *there were* fourteen persons in all.

Sons of Bilhah

The sons of *Dan*: Hushim.

The sons of *Naphtali*: Jahzeel and Guni and Jezer and Shillem.

These are the *sons of Bilhah*, whom Laban gave to his daughter Rachel, and she bore these to Jacob; *there were* seven persons in all.

All the persons belonging to Jacob, who came to Egypt, his direct descendants, *not including the wives* of Jacob's sons, *were* sixty-six persons in all, and the sons of Joseph, who were born to him in Egypt were two; all the persons of the house of Jacob, who came to Egypt, *were* seventy.

THE BLESSINGS OF JACOB TO THE TWELVE TRIBES (SONS)
(GENESIS 49)

Then Jacob summoned his sons and said, "Assemble yourselves that I may tell you what will befall you in the days to come.
"Gather together and hear, O sons of Jacob;
And listen to Israel your father.

"Reuben, you are my firstborn;
My might and the beginning of my strength, Preeminent in dignity and preeminent in power.
"Uncontrolled as water, you shall not have preeminence,
Because you went up to your father's bed;
Then you defiled it—he went up to my couch.

(Reuben's leadership position was taken away and given to Judah.)

"Simeon and Levi *are brothers;*
Their swords are implements of violence.
"Let my soul not enter into their council;
Let not my glory be united with their assembly;
Because in their anger they slew men,
And in their self-will they lamed oxen.
"Cursed be their anger, for it is fierce;
And their wrath, for it is cruel.
I will disperse them in Jacob,
And scatter them in Israel.

(The tribe of Levi, because of a redemptive act in the wilderness under
Moses, would eventually become the priesthood, and would be dispersed
among every other tribe)

"Judah, *your brothers shall praise you;*
Your hand shall be on the neck of your enemies;
Your father's sons shall bow down to you.
"Judah is a lion's whelp;
From the prey, my son, you have gone up.
He couches, he lies down as a lion,
And as a lion, who dares rouse him up?
"The scepter shall not depart from Judah,
Nor the ruler's staff from between his feet,
Until Shiloh comes, And to him shall be the obedience of the peoples.
"He ties his foal to the vine,
And his donkey's colt to the choice vine;
He washes his garments in wine,
And his robes in the blood of grapes.
"His eyes are dull from wine,
And his teeth white from milk.

(Judah would become the blood-line of Messiah and it will be from him that kings will arise. This is where we get that Jesus will be the Lion from the tribe of Judah. Because Jesus will be King the scepter will not depart from Him for all eternity. It will be His blood that will cleanse his people)

"Zebulun *will dwell at the seashore;*
And he shall be a haven for ships,
And his flank shall be toward Sidon.

"Issachar *is a strong donkey,*
Lying down between the sheepfolds.
"When he saw that a resting place was good
And that the land was pleasant,
He bowed his shoulder to bear burdens,
And became a slave at forced labor.

"Dan *shall judge his people,*
As one of the tribes of Israel.
"Dan shall be a serpent in the way,
A horned snake in the path,
That bites the horse's heels,
So that his rider falls backward.
"For Your salvation I wait, O Lord.

"As for Gad, *raiders shall raid him,*
But he will raid at their heels.

"As for Asher, *his food shall be rich,*
And he will yield royal dainties.

"Naphtali *is a doe let loose,*

He gives beautiful words.

"Joseph (through Ephraim and Manasseh) is a fruitful bough,
A fruitful bough by a spring;
Its branches run over a wall.
"The archers bitterly attacked him,
And shot at him and harassed him;
But his bow remained firm,
And his arms were agile,
From the hands of the Mighty One of Jacob
(From there is the Shepherd, the Stone of Israel),
From the God of your father who helps you,
And by the Almighty who blesses you
With blessings of heaven above,
Blessings of the deep that lies beneath,
Blessings of the breasts and of the womb.
"The blessings of your father
Have surpassed the blessings of my ancestors
Up to the utmost bound of the everlasting hills;
May they be on the head of Joseph,
And on the crown of the head of the one distinguished among his brothers.

"Benjamin is a ravenous wolf;
In the morning he devours the prey,
And in the evening he divides the spoil."

All these are the twelve tribes of Israel, and this is what their father said to them when he blessed them. He blessed them, every one with the blessing appropriate to him.

The Triumphs of Faith
(Hebrews 11 and 12:1-2)

Now faith is the assurance of things hoped for, the conviction of things not seen. For by it the men of old gained approval.

By faith we understand that the worlds were prepared by the word of God, so that what is seen was not made out of things which are visible. By faith Abel offered to God a better sacrifice than Cain, through which he obtained the testimony that he was righteous, God testifying about his gifts, and through faith, though he is dead, he still speaks.

By faith Enoch was taken up so that he would not see death; and he was not found because God took him up; for he obtained the witness that before his being taken up he was pleasing to God. And without faith it is impossible to please Him, for he who comes to God must believe that He is and that He is a rewarder of those who seek Him.

By faith Noah, being warned by God about things not yet seen, in reverence prepared an ark for the salvation of his household, by which he condemned the world, and became an heir of the righteousness which is according to faith.

By faith Abraham, *when he was called, obeyed by going out to a place which he was to receive for an inheritance; and he went out, not knowing where he was going. By faith he lived as an alien in the land of promise, as in a foreign land, dwelling in tents with Isaac and Jacob, fellow heirs of the same promise; for he was looking for the city which has foundations, whose architect and builder is God.*

By faith even Sarah *herself received ability to conceive, even beyond the proper time of life, since she considered Him faithful who had promised. Therefore there was born even of one man, and him as good as dead at that, as many descendants as the stars of heaven in number, and innumerable as the sand which is by the seashore.*

All these died in faith, without receiving the promises, but having seen them and having welcomed them from a distance, and having confessed that they were strangers and exiles on the earth. For those who say such things make it clear that they are seeking a country of their own. And indeed if they had been thinking of that country from which they went out, they would have had opportunity to return. But as it is, they desire a better country, that is, a heavenly one. Therefore God is not ashamed to be called their God; for He has prepared a city for them.

By faith Abraham, *when he was tested, offered up Isaac, and he who had received the promises was offering up his only begotten son; it was he to whom it was said, "In Isaac your descendants shall be called." He considered that God is able to raise people even from the dead, from which he also received him back as a type.*

By faith Isaac *blessed Jacob and Esau, even regarding things to come.*

By faith Jacob, *as he was dying, blessed each of the sons of Joseph, and worshiped, leaning on the top of his staff.*

By faith Joseph, *when he was dying, made mention of the exodus of the sons of Israel, and gave orders concerning his bones.*

By faith Moses, *when he was born, was hidden for three months by his parents, because they saw he was a beautiful child; and they were not afraid of the king's edict. By faith Moses, when he had grown up, refused to be called the son of Pharaoh's daughter, choosing rather to endure ill-treatment with the people of God than to enjoy the passing pleasures of sin,* considering the reproach of Christ *greater riches than the treasures of Egypt; for he was looking to the reward. By faith he left Egypt, not fearing the wrath of the king; for he endured, as seeing Him who is unseen. By faith he kept the Passover and the sprinkling of the blood, so that he who destroyed the firstborn would not touch them. By faith they passed through the Red Sea as though they were passing through dry land; and the Egyptians, when they attempted it, were drowned.*

By faith the walls of Jericho fell down after they had been encircled for seven days (Joshua).

By faith Rahab *the harlot did not perish along with those who were disobedient, after she had welcomed the spies [t]in peace.*

And what more shall I say? For time will fail me if I tell of Gideon, Barak, Samson, Jephthah, of David and Samuel *and* the prophets, *who by faith conquered kingdoms, performed acts of righteousness, obtained promises, shut the mouths of lions, quenched the power of fire, escaped the edge of the sword, from weakness were made strong, became mighty in war, put foreign armies to flight.*

Women received back their dead by resurrection; and others were tortured, not accepting their release, so that they might obtain a better resurrection; and others *experienced mockings and scourgings, yes, also chains and imprisonment. They were stoned, they were sawn in two, they were tempted, they were put to death with the sword; they went about in sheepskins, in goatskins, being destitute, afflicted, ill-treated (men of whom the world was not worthy), wandering in deserts and mountains and caves and holes in the ground.*

***And all these, having gained approval through their faith, did not receive what was promised, because God had provided something better for us, so that apart from us they would not be made perfect.

Therefore, since we have so great a cloud of witnesses surrounding us (OT believers, NT believers, modern-day believers), let us also lay aside every encumbrance and the sin which so easily entangles us, and let us run with endurance the race that is set before us, fixing our eyes on Jesus, the author and perfecter of faith, who for the joy set before Him endured the cross, despising the shame, and has sat down at the right hand of the throne of God.

BIBLIOGRAPHY

Chapter 1 –One Thousand Gifts, page 53, publisher Zondervan 2010

Chapter 3 – Statistics from George Barna article on the web, 2009, "Evangelism Si Most Effective Among Kids"

Chapter 3 – "Understanding the Teen Brain" – Health Encyclopedia, University of Rochester Medical Center – taken from the website.

Chapter 6 –"Flawless" sung by Mercy Me, Capitol Christian Music Group, Brentwood, Tn. 37027; licensing permit #589109

Chapter 7 – C.S. Lewis, The Problem of Pain, 1940 originally published by Centenbury Press, current publisher Harper Collins.

Chapter 9 – "Hungry", by Kathryn Scott, sung by Mercyme, Licensing permit #558462 Music Services, Inc.

Chapter 10 – "Overcoming Hurt" by Dr. Ralph Woerner. Published by Gospel Publishing Ass. PO Box 94368, Birmingham, Al. 35220, 1992

Chapter 11 – "Americans have little or no money saved, USA Today, March 31, 2015

Chapter 14 – "The Lion and The Lamb" song sung by Big Daddy Weave, Capitol Music License Permit #589110

Epilogue – Website, City of Shechem Today in the West Bank, August 24, 2008

Also NRB TV program, "Beyond Patterns of Evidence: The Exodus," May 12, 2016, archeology digs of a Semitic city in Egypt DVD can be bought on Amazon.

RECOMMENDED READING

1) The Bait of Satan, John Beverly, 1994, Charisma House Publishers
2) Shattering Your Strongholds, Liberty Salvarsan, 1992, Bridge Logos Publishers
3) Where Is God When It Hurts, Phillip Yancey, 2013, Zondervan Publishers
4) The Freedom Factor, Dr Bruce Wilkinson, 2016, Zeal Books
5) 7X70, Dr Bruce Wilkinson, 2016, zeal Books